I Was R

Murdoch's

Figleaf

John Bull

CHAPLIN BOOKS

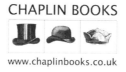

www.chaplinbooks.co.uk

First published in 2015 by Chaplin Books

ISBN 978-1-909183-69-8

A CIP catalogue record for this book is available from The British Library

Design by Michael Walsh at The Better Book Company

Printed by Imprint Digital

Chaplin Books
1 Eliza Place
Gosport PO12 4UN
Tel: 023 9252 9020
www.chaplinbooks.co.uk

I Was Rupert Murdoch's Figleaf

To Joe with best regards — it seems you were listening to my lectures after all . . .

John.

Also by John Bull

The Night They Blitzed The Ritz:
Memoirs of a Bomb-Alley Kid

The Smile on the Face of the Pig:
Confessions of the Last Cub Reporter

For Monty Levy – always on my side

FLEET STREET AND ST. PAUL'S CATHEDRAL, LONDON.

Contents

A pale ray of sunlight seeps through a dusty stained glass window to light a shabby congregation – all kneeling, hands together, eyes closed in devout prayer:

"Thank you, Lord. Thank you, thank you, thank you ... thank you for saving us ... I'll never doubt again, never never ... sweet, sweet Amen ..."

The scene is a Fleet Street pub at lunchtime – and, as yet, hardly a drop's been touched. I stand up, cross myself, dust the knees of my corduroy trousers and reach to take a grateful sip of my first-today pint of London Pride.

All around me my fellow workers are rising from their knees: men – and a few women – all known to the world as hacks, penny liars, scribbling scum, foot-in-the-door merchants, callous bastards, and reptiles. The massed hacks of the News of the World *at prayer.*

We are celebrating a crucial moment. Just ended is a long, bitter financial war involving City of London heavyweights and legal eagles. It has been the saving of the venerable 126-year-old, world-best-selling Sunday paper from the grasping hands of the monster – Robert Maxwell, who sees himself as the next Beaverbrook or Rothermere, the ruling lords of Fleet Street.

And our unlikely saviour? A green newcomer to the Fleet Street jungle, a raw young hayseed from the Australian outback: Rupert Murdoch.

1

Fifty dirty views of the world

Fleet Street was always a screaming battle for circulation figures. When I joined the *News of the World* in 1968, the paper was battling to sell four million copies a week. It was well ahead of the competition, but the more readers they got, the more the 'Treasury' (my own nickname for newspaper staff involved with the money) could charge for advertisements.

Everyone connected with the paper and its circulation – staff, shareholders, distributors and newsagents – was still bewailing the passing of the wonderful heyday in the 1950s when the paper sold eight million copies a week (no that's not a misprint, EIGHT million) and they could pretty well charge what the hell they liked for even a tiny little ad at the bottom of an inside page.

However, this huge circulation was largely a trick of the light. In World War II and the austerity years that followed, newsprint was strictly rationed. So papers were thin, microscopic compared with the hundred-plus pages of today. But the canny readers got round this by buying at least two papers on Sunday instead of just one. And whichever they preferred – *The People, the Sunday Pictorial, Sunday Despatch*, or *Empire News* – the second choice was overwhelmingly the *News of the World*.

What evidence do I have for this? Well, I had a 'paper round' when I was 12, covering a few streets in my boyhood town of Gosport in Hampshire, delivering the morning and evening papers from a bag over my shoulder. But on the Sabbath I had so many to carry that the newsagent provided me with a little cart, no more than a box on wheels.

Close examination revealed that half the papers were the *NoW*, and the rest were split between the *Sunday Pictorial* and *The People*, along with a few also-rans.

Hence the *NoW*'s magic eight million, the world's largest sale ever. To this day, to my knowledge, that has never been beaten.

Using the industry yardstick of three readers per copy this gives a grand total of 24 million. What a market! If only they'd had the newsprint for more pages to carry money-spinning ads ... but in any case 8,000,000 tuppences was not to be sniffed at either; it's about £66,000 (about six million quid in today's money) and that's every Sunday, religiously, don't forget.

The *NoW* had become the unchallenged leader of the pack because of its reputation for sex stories, or 'filth' as the staid and hypocritical English Establishment tended to call it. Of course they had to read it in order to condemn it. Or so they said.

Rugby club men up and down the country, especially public school types, are no strangers to sexual metaphor and revel in singing 'shocking' songs during beery celebrations. I became familiar with these sporting caricatures in my earliest days as a cub reporter (that's what they used to call us newspaper apprentices) when I briefly covered rugby union games in Hampshire in the 1950s.

A few of the most popular were *One Sunday in the Dockyard Church* (wonderfully scatalogical), *Beer is Best*, and *The Good Ship Venus*, (no prize for guessing the rhyme). But best of all was a song which highlighted the joys of Sunday breakfast with what the elite of the working class called the *News of the Screws.*

A couple of friends of mine used to stand on a table to perform this number – in a favourite, but out-of-the-way pub in the New Forest and after the official closing time – usually accompanied by our piano-playing genius, who would sometimes use his bare feet on the keys just to show off.

It goes to the tune of *Waiting for the Robert E Lee* ...

> *In some Sunday papers you read of the capers*
> *Of dustmen and drapers, lustmen and rapers,*
> *Girls are whipped, stripped, every foul deed is done,*
> *Lashed to the bedpost and craftily wee'd upon.*
> *A further sensation informing the nation*
> *Is gross fornication round Warren Street station*
> *In the bold old News of the World*
> *That brings you sex with your breakfast Sundays.*

> *So read your News of the World and get your facts of filth unfurled,*
> *You get your sin, sex, sodomy and sadists*
> *in the good old News of the World.*

> *Now just before Easter a lad met disaster,*
> *His local scoutmaster could run a lot faster.*
> *A farmer slept with his horse, it was a female horse of course,*
> *A chorus girl rogered by thugs, a debutante who took drugs,*
> *A young girl from Horsham, no sense of proportion,*
> *By means of contortion, contrived an abortion ...*
> *In the bold old News of the World that brings you sex with your*
> *breakfast Sundays.*

> *So read your News of the World and get your facts of filth unfurled,*
> *You get your pimps, poofs, pansies and perverters*

> *In the good old News of –*
> *Lecherous abuse of –*
> *Fifty dirty views of the World.*

Naturally these wonderful lyrics are a wild exaggeration of the contents of the *News of the World* in its heyday. I mean to say, how could that sort of thing have possibly arisen from a building that was once the home of an order of monks – the White Friars – who gave that particular slice of London its name?

I was recruited to the ranks of this world-beating newspaper in 1968 by Michael Gabbert, head of the 'Pompey Mafia' – our enterprising gang of former cub reporters on the *Portsmouth Evening News* who were now scrabbling for top jobs in Fleet Street.

Gabbert had just won the title of Reporter of the Year for his exposé for *The People* of bribery among players in the Football League and was consequently lured to the rival *NoW* by its flamboyant editor Stafford Somerfield to take on the role of assistant editor. Michael in his turn suggested that I was the sort of journalist they needed – someone who quickly grasped the way things were. Someone who was never out for Number One. A guy with a reputation for being clever, without threatening his boss – because he simply wasn't interested in being the boss.

I'd worked with Gabbert in London before, at the American news agency Associated Press, until I went to Paris as desk editor with Agence France Presse, an assignment which was cut short by having to flee civil war raging through the streets of the city over General De Gaulle's decision to give up the Algerian colonies and end a long, bitter colonial war. At the height of the troubles the Secret Army were murdering a Paris policeman every day. It wasn't a safe place for my baby daughter, Yolanda, or for my heavily pregnant wife, Robina.

I'd also worked in Fleet Street before. While Michael Gabbert was at *The People*, I'd done a Sunday shift just up the road in the features department of the *Daily Mirror* – a useful supplement to my regular job as a sub-editor on the *Southern Evening Echo* in Southampton.

Because Southampton's main line to London was out of action while it was being electrified (not before time) I'd commuted to work on the last steam trains to run from the old Ocean Liner terminus by the docks – a real joy of an old-fashioned trip through the lovely Meon Valley.

I'd had a great time at the *Mirror* as I adapted to the different skills required by the features subs. Some of the writers had been household names, but the leader of the pack had been 'Cassandra', alias Bill Connors, with his tart, sometimes excoriating thrusts at politicians or idols of the day. Bill, then recently knighted as Sir William Connors, was a legendary figure with a following of millions, much given to references and allusions to classical characters.

Somehow I had found myself sub-editing the great man's Monday column. Even the best of us needs a sub-editor to check for human error or memory failure and even Homer may nod – but it was rare for Cassandra. So it was with some trepidation that I had drawn the chief sub's attention to a slight mistake in the great man's copy.

"Give the old bugger a call then and see what he says," he'd told me. " But double check with the library first, eh?"

Of course I'd already checked with the *Mirror*'s inexhaustible reference systems, so I made the call.

The butler had answered: "Sir William Connor's residence."

"It's the office – is Sir William available?"

Then the unmistakable growl ...

"Who's that?"

"It's John Bull in the subs, Sir William."

"Ah, John – when it's the paper, call me Bill, OK? What have I got wrong now?"

I had explained.

"Well spotted. That's a pint I owe you when I see you in the pub."

After that, of course, I had been given his column to read every Sunday. But I don't recall ever winning another pint.

So Michael Gabbert persuaded Stafford Somerfield to give me a chance. And he warned me: "Whatever he says, don't argue with him."

There's always some little frisson in the air when people meet for the first time. As I entered his spacious office, Stafford – an imposing figure with a fine show of white hair, a broad smile and a knowing eye – came towards me arm extended to shake hands and I saw at once he had a couple of fingers missing from his right hand, just like Len Collings, my first newspaper boss. So, I was ready to smile and grasp the sound hand with no awkwardness at all.

"Grenade?" I asked.

Stafford showed no surprise. "Yes, Italy, World War II."

"My first boss had the same wound," I told him. "In the 14-18 rehearsal."

Start of a beautiful friendship

From there the interview went well. He talked about his vision for the *News of the World* and asked about my days at the news agencies. We were comfortable with each other, and he was ready to give me a chance to show what I could do.

Then the money came up.

Stafford sat down and leafed through some papers on his desk – finally he said: "I can offer you £2,000 a year."

"Make it guineas?" I suggested.

Gabbert rolled his eyes. Stafford sighed, looked straight at me, then, after the longest pause ...

"Okay. Now get out before I change my mind."

His letter confirming my appointment arrived a couple of days later:

Dear John,

Thank you for coming in to see us on Thursday. I thoroughly enjoyed our chat.

I now write to confirm your starting date with us as Tuesday, April 23, 1968.

I believe it must be a good omen for John Bull to be joining the News of the World on St George's Day and William Shakespeare's birthday.

Good Luck,

Stafford.

Well I did stay there for nearly 20 years.

2

In the Big Room

For the English paper with the world's biggest circulation, the *News of the World* had a remarkably small staff. Bear with me while I introduce the leading figures – the ones who produced this 'torrent of filth' every Sunday.

NOYES THOMAS – Foreign correspondent

Noyes Thomas, known in the Street as 'Tommy,' was acknowledged by his rivals as one of the best of Britain's foreign correspondents.

In World War II he joined the Gurkhas and served in the Far East, ending up as a lieutenant colonel on the staff of Lord Mountbatten.

He returned to the *NoW* and covered most of the newsworthy foreign stories for another couple of decades. Tommy was named after the poet Alfred Noyes, his uncle, but he soon dropped the 'Alfred.' A newcomer once asked him in El Vino, our Fleet Street winebar, how many countries he'd worked in. Tommy sighed. "Most of them, actually, except for some of the remoter parts of Mongolia."

PETER EARLE – Crime reporter

In those days, the *NoW* was universally noted for its coverage of the underworld, in which it was rivalled only by *The People*. Peter broke the Christine Keeler-Profumo scandal-in-high-places that has often been blamed for the fall of the Tory government of the day. He also had a unique reputation for great opening lines with our customers.

When a landlady demanded: 'How do I know you are Peter Earle of the News of the World?', Peter told her: 'Look, I've just admitted it.'

Despatched to Rome with orders to persuade the Earl of Warwick to talk about 'domestic' problems at home, Peter tracked his man down to a golf course outside the Eternal City. Dressed in a long cloak which flapped about him as he strode across the green, Peter approached the nobleman and his coterie, and went straight into Shakespeare mode:

"My Lord of Warwick, a great storm gathers about you in England!"

And so he got his story.

He and our other crime specialist Charles Sandell (nickname Charlie Scandal, of course) were household names to most people in the UK.

FRANK BUTLER – Sports editor

Next up: Frank Butler, Fleet Street's best-known and longest-serving sports editor. His father James was boxing correspondent at the *Daily Herald* and introduced him to some of the old-time greats of the square ring.

At 16 Frank joined the *Daily Express* as a junior and at 18 was reporting boxing and football under his own by-line. At 24 he was made sports editor of the *Sunday Express.*

In 1949 the *NoW* hired Butler as sports columnist on a salary to match the best-selling paper. He became sports editor in 1960.

REG DRURY – Soccer pundit

The *NoW* sports desk included Reg Drury, a walking football encyclopaedia and skilled assessor of football talent. He was also a welcome addition to any dinner table. He told me once he never had a problem hailing a taxi – drivers kept an eye open for him just so they could put him right about his view of their heroes last Saturday.

'PEGASUS' – Racing pundit

Chief racing correspondent was the amiable Pegasus, aka Stan Agate, often at the top of the Fleet Street tipsters' league table and a joyful companion at the tracks, where he had the ear of every owner, trainer, jockey, bookie, punter and barman, and, it was rumoured, even some of the ponies.

He used to organise trips to the world-famous Arc de Triomphe race at Longchamp on the first Sunday in October. Ah, Paris in the autumn! It being a day off for Sunday-paper slaves, we were often there in numbers.

WESTON TAYLOR – Showbiz

Weston Taylor was a quiet man, but was also the showbiz man every actor, comedian or singer wanted to call friend. Praise from Weston could be a career-maker.

DAVID ROXAN – Industrial correspondent

The redoubtable David Roxan covered the voices of the trade unions and general left-leaning organisations and he was once described to me by a Scottish Labour supporter as 'Aboot the only honest reporter in th' bloody world.'

'GEORGE EDWARDS' – Foreign editor

A middle-aged chap of continental charm and accent, George Edwards covered anything he could translate from the (mainly) European press. He also wrote a regular column about card games – and every Christmas invented a new card game for the readers.

No one knew his original nationality or his real name, but he wrote under the patriotic by-line – a combination of two recent kings – George Edwards.

CHARLIE MARKUS – News editor

Charlie Markus was arguably the best ever news editor – his team of staff reporters was small but beautifully led. And Charlie defended them from criticism as savagely as any mother bear with cubs. He had them all singing from the same hymn sheet – backed by a choir of talented freelances and court reporters up and down the country.

Furthermore, in all the times I spent in the pubs with Charlie's angels I never, ever heard any of them seriously run their boss down.

Charlie could take a joke, too. In my early days we were having an office party in The Golf Club (nowhere near a golf course, but just round the corner from the *NoW* – it was actually a nice pub and served decent snacks). Wives were invited and so Robina came up from Southampton.

I only left her for a few minutes – to pop over to Mick's café in Fleet Street to stock up on some Gitanes ... well maybe a bit longer. When I got back the party was warming up a bit, but Charlie was giving me some funny looks.

"Charlie Markus seems to be giving me the fisheye," I confided to my beloved.

"Yeah, that'd be right," she said. "After you left me, Charlie came over:

'Whose wife are you then?'
'I'm Robina, John Bull's wife, Charlie.'
'How come you know my name?'
(Cue caricature north country accent)
' I recognised yer from me 'oosband's imitations.'

I was actually surprised at how thin on the ground the *NoW* was compared with what seemed to me to be vast numbers of people on daily papers. At the *Mirror* for instance, there always seemed to be dozens of people wandering about or chatting on the phone.

At the *NoW* the tip-tapping of a typewriter was a fairly rare background noise, even in the highly productive reporters' room, a separate department down the corridor from the editor's office. There weren't that many reporters, and they were all men, apart from Rosalie Shann who had a huge following among the readers. Rosalie was a freelance, but she worked from the *NoW* premises.

The heart of the paper was the Big Room ... a vast expanse and a high ceiling, disappearing in a heavy fug of smoke from fags, cigars and pipes, and taking up most of the building's first floor. Planned and decorated like the set of a Hollywood Ink Opera, it even had a glassed-off area in one corner where Gabbert's investigations team worked in splendid isolation.

On Saturdays – Press Day – the Big Room buzzed like a beehive when the 'casuals' arrived. All over the country, blokes who worked daily for evening and weekly papers gobbled down a hasty Saturday breakfast, kissed their wives and kids and headed by car or rail to Fleet Street (or to satellite offices in Manchester or Dublin) to earn a handful of guineas to help the family budget. Not just for the *News of*, but for all the other Sunday papers too.

Strategically placed in the middle of the room was the subs' table. There was a desk at one end for the chief sub, Ron Lawrence, and a couple of seats either side – one of them for the newcomer: me.

Most of the page-layout and design work was carried out by George Anfield, a typical Scouser. George's sidekick Mike Brennan combined being features editor with a series of roles, including doing book reviews. Other features pages were edited by Freddie Hodgson and his assistant David Gordois, who edited the readers' letters page.

Near the subs' table was a large desk occupied by the copy boys, one in his sixties, though he denied it, and the other pushing forty. They were the backbone of the outfit – regularly brewing tea or coffee and nipping out to get things for us, especially smokes. And emptying the ashtrays regularly.

In the beginning I was placed at the end of the subs' table, as befits a makee-learn with a long way to go.

The work meant taking the raw copy from the reporters (and I do mean raw) and turning it into readable and interesting stories. We were expected to invent catchy headlines, though these were often altered by the layout men at the Friday page-make-up sessions with Stafford. The stories came in, for the most part, badly typed. We'd put them to one side and then rewrite them completely, by hand, onto octavo paper, adding the paragraph marks. Almost every story needed rewriting (ones that came from Noyes Thomas were the exception) and the reporters used to complain all the time that their copy was unrecognisable by the time we'd finished with it. Of course, if we were subbing a piece sent in by the Archbishop of Canterbury, or by Winston Churchill's son Randolph – by no means an unusual occurrence: I remember commissioning a powerful piece for the leader page from the archbishop of the day for £700 cash, for church funds of course – we'd just correct their English and leave the rest. We knew the rules of diplomacy.

When we were satisfied with a story, we handed the copy to chief sub Ron Lawrence, a lean, tallish chap in his early fifties. He had started out aiming for a career in showbiz and – if memory serves – he opened as the lead in a production of *Charley's Aunt*, the play where a public school lad poses as his visiting auntie from Brazil – the place where the other nuts come from. World War II intervened and Ron served in the RAF. He had a wonderful yarn about being in the crew of a Halifax bomber on exercise over East Anglia – they inadvertently found themselves joining a large fleet of bombers forming up over the Wash. Luckily they managed to get out of the formation – the others were all off to join the bloody mayhem of the battle of Arnhem. Ron's war wound came when he fell out of the plane after they landed. He had suffered with a bad back ever since.

His right-hand man was Monty Levy. Monty was very fond of the salt beef and latkes at Bloom's, the Whitechapel restaurant where he was surprised at the quality of service which seemed to be reserved for him alone. He only had to raise an eyebrow for a waiter to rush to his side.

It was only later that he found out that they had mistaken him for columnist and critic Bernard Levin.

Monty (third from right) and me (in the foreground) with colleagues at The Latin Quarter

Monty was a genius who could tell any story in 25 words and leave nothing out. He still holds the record for the best *News of the World* headline of all time:

The welfare officer's nudist wife and the Chinese hypnotist from the Co-op bacon factory

The headline became famous and has been written about many times since, but they never get the wording quite right, always falling into the trap of trying to over-explain the story, such as 'The welfare officer's nudist wife *who fell for* the Chinese hypnotist at the Co-op bacon factory.' The true joy of Monty's original is its beautiful and intriguing economy. It would gladden the heart of any academic literary critic – say, for instance, F R Leavis, the exalted Cambridge don who rejoiced in deep analysis of an author's text.

To this day you are likely to come across a bloke in a pub who will, at the drop of a hat, take out his wallet and show you his treasured clipping from that paper, faded, grey with age, but still stunning.

What that guy won't know is that when Stafford, Michael Gabbert, and I were weighing up the court pages on the Friday night and congratulating Monty, he rubbed his chin – a characteristic gesture – and said: "Well, Stafford, there was another angle to the story – in that the Chinaman also had a wooden leg."

Stafford shook his head ... "Nah Monty, that would be going right over the top."

Once, doing a rewrite in my early days, I overlooked a reporter's shifting of Falmouth from Cornwall to Devon. And the other subs never let me forget it.

"Don't trust him," they'd say in the pub. "He's shit at geography."

And do you know, all those years later – on the day I left the *NoW* – someone actually made an impromptu speech: "He may not have been too bad as a sub – except his geography was shit. He once moved Falmouth from Cornwall to Devon."

This meticulous accuracy of the *News of the World* in all things may come as something of a surprise.

Of course, it's easy to make a mistake when you're under pressure. I recall the day on the *Southern Evening Echo* when we'd got the paper out, but there was still the *Football Echo* to finish. The subs were heads down, slaving away as they tried to unravel a piece phoned in by some past-it old timer – or worse, from some kid hoping to get into ink. The door from the Reporters Room had suddenly swung open and reporter Don Osmond, (also the paper's cartoonist, 'Oz') had hurried up to the top of the table to Jimmy Clay, deputy chief sub.

"Do us a favour, mate," he'd said, shoving a handful of copy into Jimmy's tray. "Can you get this in the paper for Monday? I should have put it in earlier, but I was busy."

With a sigh Jimmy had picked up the copy and waved Oz away. "Clear off – I've got an edition to get out!"

But of course he did sub the story and shoved it, along

with Oz's cartoon, into the printer's tray sometime later. And that, folks, is how the city of Southampton and about half of Hampshire got their first review of the Church of England's brand new 1961 edition of the Holy Bible, complete with an oversize drop letter 'T' at the start – an all-too-graphic illustration of naked Adam as a wickedly grinning old satyr chasing a tasty-looking Eve round a palm tree. I heard later that copies of that paper were being sold on the streets on Monday at two bob a copy. Oz had got a right rollicking from the management and we'd all gone on our merry way.

When I took up my duties on the subs' table at the *NoW* I apparently amazed my colleagues by telling them I lived in Southampton and travelled back and forth by train every day.

'Well he won't be with us long,' they said. 'He won't be able to cope with commuting every day – it must be more than 70 miles.'

But then I asked them how long it took them. And none of the subs could beat my door-to-door trip of 70 minutes for the train and a stroll over Waterloo Bridge and down Fleet Street to Bouverie Street.

Ron Lawrence always managed to get in first from Esher and he used to frown at me. So I took evasive action. One day he made some comment about my 'late arrivals' and I was happy to show him my little diary – with tiny stars against the working days.

"See these little stars, Ron?" I asked him. "Each one represents one of the subs coming in after me. Lots of them, aren't there?"

The topic never was mentioned again. Who would want to be my boss, eh?

Thing was, the line had just been electrified and had all the latest gear to speed things up – and in those days my 9.10am to Waterloo made only one stop, at Winchester. Furthermore, being a new line meant it wasn't very busy – I often had a whole carriage to myself coming in. And there was a very welcome bar service in the diner going home. Later I'll tell you how that bit made my job more interesting and actually brought me in a steady supply of exclusive stories. Besides, subs and layout men only worked from Wednesday to Saturday. I used to draw a line down the calendar every month with work days coloured a dark blue and home days coloured red – plenty of time to spend at home with my wife and our delightful daughters, Yolanda and Rosemary.

A very Edwardian family

Of the subs, Ron Lawrence and Monty lived in commuterville in Surrey, and Ted Harriott out in the wilds of Suffolk. Another sub, Laurie Andrews, took me home with him a couple of times – a slow train ride and a four-mile trek across the farmland that bordered his dormitory village. It got more ludicrous later when we were joined by Dixon Scott, a writer I'd met in my subbing shifts at the *Daily Mirror* where he specialised in entertaining comic pieces. He commuted in from his small farm in deep country somewhere in the eastern counties. In wintry weather it must have felt like the Steppes of Russia out there.

They still persisted in regarding Southampton as being out in the sticks, though strangely in the 60s it could be more accurately described as being a satellite of New York – a slice of the Big Apple. This was because the great ocean liners, principally the Queen Mary and the Queen Elizabeth, were still the floating hotels of choice for crossing what the locals on both sides called the Herring Pond.

Many Southampton families had a relative or two serving on the liners, or working the waterfront on either side. It was not at all unusual to meet blokes in a pub who spoke with a damn-near-authentic Brooklyn drawl, a bit like Marlon Brando in Elia Kazan's unforgettable *On the Waterfront*.

Fleet Street paid homage to this phenomenon by planting staff reporters in Southampton, or 'stringers' (freelances with a steady contract). So in the pubs we journos favoured, I often found myself in the company of John Sandiford (*Daily Express)*, Frank Cooper (*Daily Mirror* photographer), Brian Freemantle (*London Evening News* and later *Daily Express*), Bill Dolby (*Daily Herald*), plus a couple of freelances that included George Clogg (*Daily Mail*) and Peter Wightman, a stringer for the *Daily Sketch.*

For news pictures there were also the local father-and-son photographers Jim and Chris Wood, constantly battling with each other – as is customary in such a cut-throat career. Except once, when a stevedore fell from the deck of the Queen Mary as the great liner was docking. Instantly, Jim and Chris both took off their coats and dived to the rescue. Luckily the *Daily Echo* man got pictures of the drama, sold them to the national papers and gave the proceeds to the heroes. And they were both awarded a medal for bravery.

You think that ended the scrapping? Not a chance. With the week they were at each other's throats again.

When I had worked at the *Echo*, the paper's two star turns – Tony Brode, poet and regular contributor to *Punch*, the nation's up-market comic for the cogniscenti, and John Edgar Mann, encyclopedic expert on films and noted folk and jazz guru – both enthusiastically led the movement that played up to this Yankee obsession. They ran a story that the hit song *The Bells of St Mary's* – a great success for the Old Groaner Bing Crosby in the film *Going my Way* – was 'proven' to have been written by a visiting guy from Tin Pan Alley inspired (so to speak) by a peal from Southampton's own Mother Church of St Mary's.

The Fleet Street gang had a standing invitation from Cunard's PR agency to greet all incoming star passengers in his, or her, stateroom when the ship docked at Southampton. One not-too-bright freelance reporter, standing in for a staff man, was thrilled to be able to ask a question of gorgeously dressed Pearl Bailcy, best remembered for her knockout performance as Frankie in the all-black film *Carmen Jones*, and possessor of an armful of awards for so many hit songs.

Pearl with Jimmy Durante

Reporter: "Miss Bailey, would you describe your coat as nigger brown?"

She didn't bat an eyelid: "Not where I come from, honey."

Years later I was commissioned to interview the great scientist and sci-fi writer Isaac Asimov on board Queen Elizabeth 2 when she docked. I did my homework beforehand and noting that he was fond of female company, I borrowed a friend's wife to come with me as my assistant.

We were both shown into his stateroom, where he was sipping coffee and looking just like any other bloke feeling a bit bored with sea travel, despite the luxury liner. But he brightened up immediately he saw the lovely Eileen – and I don't think he took his eyes off her at all.

"Tell me, sir," I started, "you are on record as stating that you would never leave Manhattan ... and here you are ..."

The wily old bugger then winked at Eileen, raised himself up in his chair and peered out the porthole.

"Mister, I may have been lied to and possibly kidnapped – please tell me this boat is still tied up at Pier 90 on the East River."

At this point the cabin door opened and a spotty young chap carrying a microphone and recorder announced that he was from the BBC. I would have advised him to get lost, but Asimov beckoned him in and told him to sit down.

Things got worse when he pulled out a notebook and said: "Can I just check the spelling of your name, sir?"

I wanted to throttle the kid – but Asimov and Eileen were both doubled over trying not to laugh out loud. I ask you – was he going to spell out the famous writer's name over the air?

I'd never worked on a Sunday paper before – so I had a lot to learn. So would anyone from any other paper – the *NoW* was essentially different. It highlighted the failings of the famous, the nasty little habits of the working classes, the mistakes of the politicians, and the callousness of the rich, especially the idle rich. It revered the exploits of sportsmen (and horses) and highlighted the working man's sports – darts and snooker – by setting up tournaments with attractive prizes.

In my time the crime reporters on the *NoW* used to say that they had put more members of the clergy behind bars for 'interfering' with young lads than anyone else had.

The *NoW* offered priceless advice to response to readers' problems, especially financial ones, in its peerless Hilton Bureau column, a totally altruistic venture originally set up by John Hilton, who was born in 1880 when England still had its share of 'dark satanic mills.' Hilton had been an apprenticed mechanic. He had later gone to study in Russia and in the 1930s had become Cambridge professor of industrial relations. Until World War II, he had also written a regular column for the *News Chronicle* and then broadcast on the BBC advising listeners on their rights. In March 1942 the *NoW* had hired him to carry on the work for its readers, but he died in 1943. The column was then changed to the 'Hilton Bureau', offering legal and similar advice to readers from a battery of specialists. Week after week, the *NoW* reported the cudgels the bureau had taken up to deal with backsliding firms or nationalised industry and its fair share of jumped-up Little Hitlers.

We also ran a very popular Ladies' Fashions competition which headlined the centrefold and offered worthwhile prizes (I know 'cos my mum had won at least twice in the 1950s).

Some of the old favourites we kept – years later, despite its drive to sophistication, the *NoW* was still running a Wedding Anniversaries column. Very popular with older readers, it was a weekly list of names sent in by wives all over the country who were proud to have their anniversary recognised in the world's biggest newspaper.

To give people a taste of what having millions of readers really means, I like to quote the story of a young ex-RAF man who, towards the end of World War II on one of his last operations, was given a parachute which he discovered had a note tucked into the fabric: "packed with love and best wishes, Brenda West."

He kept the note, figuring it would bring him luck, and a year or so after his demob he found it among his bits and pieces. His pals at the pub put him up to writing to the *News of the World* asking if Brenda was still around. Of course it duly appeared on our letters page, where it was spotted by at least two friends of Brenda. Inevitably the *NoW* sent reporters to cover the reunion – and a few months later carried a happy picture of the couple's wedding.

3

The Sun-Dappled Sub

My own assessment of the *NoW* – as I had worked out in my youth – was that people took the paper to find out, by the examples quoted in its human stories, a yardstick against which to measure their own behaviour; what was allowed and what was punished, and covering most of the in-between ... anything that was held up to ridicule. Most of the copy the subs handled was the product of courts up and down the land – any place, in fact, where there had a been what the snobbish critics called 'filth', a case with sexual connotations.

On the subs' table with me, Monty Levy and Ted Harriott was a younger chap who had joined not long before me – Laurie Andrews, known as Lol, who had earned the nickname 'the sun-dappled sub'. This was because in his rewrite of some court reporter's copy he had started with a lyrical setting to contrast with the horrors of an attack on a young girl.

I won't attempt to do it as lyrically as Lol – but it might go something like this:

> A riverbank dotted with wild violets, under the shade of a willow tree ... the sun gently flickering through the green foliage, sparkling on the water of a shallow brook, the bubbling of the stream mingling with the sweet twittering of birds.
>
> Wendy, a 16-year-old shop assistant, lay back on the bank, reading her copy of *Tender Love Stories* ...

Then came the evidence in the court report and the stout denial of the youth, or often a much older bloke, the villain of the piece. There were also the comments of the lawyers, prosecuting or defending, and finally the summing-up of the judge – often including a shaft or two of courtroom wit.

The court cases we dealt with ranged from indecent assault to outright rape – not that that word ever figured in the story. The nearest we got was 'interfered with' or 'a serious assault occurred.' In one typical story the girl was said to have been 'cruelly battered about the face and body ... *but she had not been molested.*'

Often we used a standard introduction when the defendant pleaded not guilty: 'Two very different versions of what happened next were told to Portsmouth Magistrates ...'

And – believe it or not – that was the formula for what the *NoW*'s critics called 'filth'.

Here's a typical headline and intro from my early-days scrapbook:

A MAN ON THE BONNET
IN LOVERS' LANE

News of the World Reporter

The common by night was a favourite rendezvous for courting couples ... Among those who enjoyed its peace was a sergeant in the Special Constabulary and his girl friend. While the sergeant was sitting in his car with his girl friend he noticed, to his amazement, a man lying on the bonnet and looking through the windscreen.

So the story began ... and it ended with a peeping tom found guilty in court and jailed for six months.

Ron Lawrence made it clear to me that everything had to be checked and double-checked. If it didn't suit him, it went straight on the spike. The subs were expert at identifying the top lawyers – from the legal *Who's Who* books stacked on the table between us. Get a lawyer's name wrong and you were in trouble. Get a judge's name wrong and you might as well stroll round to Wormwood Scrubs and bang yourself up. Newspaper career over.

In those days lawyers were forbidden to advertise. They wanted their names in the '*Screws*' so the villains and the solicitors would know who to hire – and that's how it was until Margaret Thatcher became the buggers' best friend by allowing them to stick their names up in lights. They've become more and more blatant since – already in one local street market I stumbled on an enterprising shyster who'd set up a tent advertising legal advice – "Had an accident? – Let us advise you, while you wait." I get the feeling that it won't be long before solicitors sponsor the black marias taking the villains to and from court. A banner on the side of the van might read ...

> *"Another Bunch of Yobs Getting Away With It, Thanks to Winsom, Quibble and Petty, of Old Bailey. No Win, No Fee.'*

Talking of the Scrubs – locked in there you would, of course, be a member of a very select bunch of convicts, many of whom owed their presence there to the good old *NoW.* Here's just a few (courtesy of *Famous Prisoners of Wormwood Scrubs* by Stephen Wade):

- Paul Blackburn, who served 25 years for a crime he didn't commit
- George Blake, the most famous spy of them all
- Horatio Bottomley, swindler, playboy and owner (ironically) of *John Bull* magazine and *The Sun*
- Charles Bronson, not the film star but the London gangster, who spent so long in jails that he wrote *The Good Prison Guide*
- Fred Copeman, political scrapper and organiser of picketing on behalf of the National Unemployed Workers' Movement

- Pete Doherty and Keith Richards, both rock stars imprisoned for drugs offences
- Lord Alfred Douglas, ('Bosie'), lover of Oscar Wilde, banged up for libel against Winston Churchill
- Nicholas van Hoogstraten, racketeer who even managed to run his business from inside the prison walls
- Thomas Jones, later Baron Maelor, and poet Basil Bunting, both conscientious objectors in The Great War
- Saunders Lewis and Lewis Valentine, Welsh nationalists who burnt down an RAF training school
- Konon Molody, a Russian spy who posed as jukebox salesman Gordon Lonsdale
- Count Geoffrey Potocki de Montalk, writer of obscene poems
- Karel Richter, German spy
- Nikos Sampson, editor of the *Times* of Cyprus, and fighter for the independence of Cyprus from Britain
- Richard Starkie, Harley Street abortionist
- John Stonehouse, politician and fraudster who faked his own death
- Michael Tippett, classical musician who joined the Peace Pledge Union and refused to serve in the Second War War
- Peter Wildblood, *Daily Mail* journalist, jailed – along with Lord Montagu, for being a homosexual
- and – courtesy of the *Dandy* comic – Korky the Cat (see page 74)

Lol showed me the finer points of the job and introduced me to the pubs the *NoW* used, the top bar of the Tipperary being chiefly the haunt of our reporters, and the Punch Tavern the resort of the subs and features team. Each newspaper had its favourite pub, but occasionally would welcome a pal from down the street – though they never talked about their stories. When I'd worked Sunday shifts on the *Daily Mirror*, a favourite lunch venue had been The Gay Hussar, and in fine weather we used to picnic on delicacies ordered in from Bloom's, sending a cabbie to Whitechapel to fetch them back to our picnic ground – often St Mary's Church, Aldermanbury, the one they were pulling down stone by stone, each one clearly marked and numbered for shipping to Fulton, Missouri, where the whole church now stands rebuilt, exactly as was.

St Mary's had connections with Shakespeare and his bust stands in the pleasant garden now on the site. It's also the last resting (uneasily resting, I hope) place of the notorious seventeenth-century Judge Jeffries, the 'hanging judge.'

Lol introduced me to the journalists' church of St Bride, the one that looks like a three-tier wedding cake, situated along the alleyway behind the Old Bell, another Fleet Street hostelry, mainly used by casuals working for the *NoW* on Saturdays. He also persuaded me to join the St Bride Institute which had a library, a games room and a swimming pool. Now and again we'd have a swim. We also used the library – and Laurie introduced me to avant garde novelists B S Johnson and J G Farrell, both of whom took their own lives while still in their forties.

St Bride's – the 'wedding cake' church

He could be volatile – he once poured a pint of beer over a paparazzo photographer (one of the first to bear the name) who was annoying some of our colleagues in the pub.

Michael Gabbert was so impressed by this that he offered to pay for Lol's drinks for a week. He came to stay with me in Southampton a couple of times and we used to sail my little dinghy 'Pry' up and down the River Hamble. On one occasion we were attacked by half a dozen canoes from the youth holiday camp on the river – canoes manned by German girls. One adventurous group got too near and splashed half the river over us with their paddles. Lol took off his shirt and trousers, dived into the river and swam menacingly towards them ... when they saw he meant business they paddled like crazy in the vague direction of Hamburg.

The subs and features department had the air of a London gentleman's club, with a solid fug of smoke rising from a battery of ashtrays down the middle of the table – gentlemanly that is, apart from the occasional outbreak of artistic temperament, such as the time when two of us subs became involved in an arcane argument that ended with me pinning the other guy down on the desktop with a copy spike through his shirt collar. An incident dismissed by our colleagues as 'all part of the game, old boy.'

A network of court reporters on local papers or working for agencies throughout Britain kept the *NoW* regularly supplied with any story with a trace of s-e-x.

And then there were the divorce cases.

The passing of the 1937 Divorce Act allowing divorce on the ground of adultery for either partner led to a bonanza of new dirty stories for the *Screws*. The law didn't allow use of the actual evidence, so reporters had to rely on the facts as provided by the judge's summing up.

If a couple wanted to divorce, the most popular and fuss-free method was for the husband to be caught *in flagrante delicto*.

Actually the new law also meant more business for private detectives and the women they hired. The usual drill was for the husband to book into a hotel (Brighton was very popular) where he would be joined by a young woman. Later a private detective would nip in and snatch a flash photo of the couple in bed together.

The customary phrase in the *News of the World* for this exciting and stimulating bit of filth was 'intimacy then occurred.' Oh Lor, how my knees tremble at the mere mention of the phrase. It almost ranks with the rare glimpse of my grannie's corsets which used to set my pulse racing when I was about 12.

Here's a typical example of a story that would have got the readers' pulses racing (again from my scrapbook):

'CAD'S CAR' PASSED A JUDGE'S LOVE TEST

In reply to a wife's plea for a decree on the ground of adultery, her husband had said he could not have committed misconduct in the car because it had bucket seats.

After inspecting an MGB sports car outside his court the Divorce Judge ruled: "I do not think that lovemaking in the car was impossible."

The judge decreed that the car was of a type that used to be described as a "cad's car" and duly granted a decree to the wife.

My earlier newspaper employers had been customarily a hard-faced crew, but the *NoW* was owned by the Carr family and they were an exception through their more generous habits.

The entire editorial staff were treated to a free dinner on Saturdays, in two shifts – after the first edition at 6pm and the second at 8pm. This was taken in a bar-restaurant called Dino at the Printer's Pie (better known as 'The Peanut Parlour'), which was staffed chiefly by Sicilians. Later their leader, Mario, took over premises next door and opened as The First Edition. As a reminder of earlier days, the dining room at 'The Peanut Parlour' had framed pages of the *NoW* on the walls. The earliest, about 1840, declared:

BABY'S BODY FOUND PICKLED IN JAR

Some years later I was instrumental in getting the franchise for the Saturday dinners moved to Mario's, which might account for the fact that for many years of my life my Saturday menu was:

Potted shrimp on toast
Steak au poivre, served with broccoli and small potatoes
A hardy Italian red (ah, the memory of Barbera de Piemonte!)

Michael Gabbert, always keen to make an impression on visitors and to look after his team of freelances, had come up with a wonderful arrangement with the staff at The Cheshire

 Cheese. The Cheese had been founded so long ago – probably back in Caxton's day – that it had no licence to serve food and drink. Somehow, over time, this had become the norm at the pub, but as a sort of *quid pro quo* the place had to close to the public at 9pm.

On the top floor of the ancient old building – rebuilt after the Great Fire

of London – was the boardroom, used mostly for meetings over lunch, with a better style of service and menu. Gabbert had been taken there by Stafford and typically, afterwards had a quiet word with the head waiter. The upshot was that from time to time, he would phone just before midday, and if no-one had booked the boardroom, he and his team could have a decent lunch at a cut rate. Typically, I recall, we would order some hors d'oeuvres to share, then go straight for the Scotch beef with the trimmings – plus a decent bottle of the house wine – and strawberries and cream for dessert, all for about 30 shillings a head, plus a tip for the staff.

Another early insight into Bouverie Street's cosy world was an invitation to chairman Sir William Carr's birthday party when the entire staff were invited on our Monday off, to strawberries and cream (and gallons of wine) at the governor's mansion in Sussex. It was a three-line-whip: questions were asked if you didn't show up.

NoW reporter Roy Stockdill reports in his reminiscences *The News of the World Story* that at one office function a showbiz reporter, very drunk, grabbed the chairman by the tie, banged his head against the wall and uttered the immortal question "Why are you so fucking rich and I'm so fucking poor?" Next morning, with a vague memory of what he'd done, he appeared at Bouverie Street expecting to pick up his cards. He walked into the lift, straight into the arms of Sir William. The amiable knight simply shook his head and said: "Why do we do these things?"

Now and again we'd have an editorial party – usually in the basement of The Cheshire Cheese – known as a 'Leg of Mutton Supper', a charming hang-over from the earliest days of the paper when most of the work was done by casual hacks. In order that they stay sober enough to do their work, they were treated to a free supper by the paper's owner.

It was all very different to my days on the *Southern Evening Echo*, where the only perk had been a 'tied' flat, at a peppercorn rent of about £2 a week. The job had not been too demanding and Southampton was a pleasant city for a couple with a young family. Robina and I loved walking with our little girls on the huge and beautiful Southampton Common with its famous old cemetery, a wildlife riot of squirrels, stray cats, foxes, hedgehogs, swallows and tits, nightingales after dark, and bats by the colony, set alongside a big lake with its own islands, sanctuary for all kinds of wild waterfowl.

We'd browse among its tombstones, a panorama of Edwardian and Victorian sagas often decorated by statues of angels, and little stone babies on the graves of infants untimely gone away. A misty recollection of Dickensian days; a silent, still landscape of yesterday people – figures from local government, heroes of battles against foreign armies, or struggles with roaring seas and life-swallowing waves, remembrances of lovers fled away, and of dictators fleeing with the nation's treasure and finding asylum in the great port of Southampton. Like, for instance, the runaway Juan Manuel de Rosas, dictator of Argentina. Kicked out in 1852, he fled to Southampton where he lived in some style until his death in 1877. His last resting place is still the most ornate monument in the cemetery. In 1985 Argentine

sympathisers had his bones returned to Buenos Aires, but three years earlier, during the Falklands War, someone placed a fresh wreath on the tomb. The story made the national media – "Who could have so insulted our brave boys at war with the 'Argies'?"

The best tomb in the graveyard

We hardened newspaper hacks had nodded wisely over our drinks and sagely wondered which one of us had the bright idea of sticking a wreath on the tomb and pocketing his fee for the scoop. And why hadn't we thought of it first?

The money on the *Echo* hadn't been bad: I used to get about £25 a week, plus some steady freelance income, and by the end of a year I'd saved enough for a deposit on a house and we had been able to give up our grace-and-favour flat and buy a typical Southampton Edwardian villa with spacious rooms for our growing family (our son, Michael, had been born in 1966), a decent-sized garden and a drive-in for our old car – a 1930s Austin Ten, a gift from Tony Hooke, freelance photographer and old pal.

One of the highlights when we'd lived in the flat had been our New Year's Eve parties, held in conjunction with the couple who lived upstairs, *Echo* journalist Mike Ford and his wife Gabby. Food had never been a problem with Gabby – her Italian father was butler to a grand family in Hampshire's Meon Valley, so exotic stuff like pheasant and duck were to be had in abundance and our shed and fuel store at the rear of the house had always been stocked up with logs.

When we were sending out invitations for our first New Year's Eve bash I'd had the idea that the cast of the panto at Southampton's ancient Gaumont theatre might be interested – better than sharing a few bottles of brown ale in your digs (in those days, with a matinée next day there was no way to nip home for the night). The sixties was the age of the Pop Star Panto – Cliff Richard headed a glittering cast in *Cinderella*, Frank Ifield was in *Babes in the Wood*, Engelbert Humperdink was Robinson Crusoe, Cilla Black played *Red Riding Hood*, Julie Andrews and Max Bygraves did *Cinderella* (with Jon Pertwee playing an Ugly Sister) and Ronnie Hilton sang his heart out alongside Les Dawson in *Babes in the Wood*.

Of course our parties had tended to get the support acts rather than the stars, but I do recall singing *Auld Lang Syne* with Joe 'Mr Piano' Henderson obliging on our antique piano. Local bands had also dropped in, the best of which was the gloriously named Gutta Percha's Elastic Band.

One of the best parties had involved the young cast of *Cinderella* – it was such a good party, I can't now recall who came as it left a bit of a blur. I do recall waking up on the floor as daylight sneaked through a gap in the curtains. There were people curled up all over the furniture, and as I got up, a crumpled musician had arisen from behind the sofa clutching his saxophone.

Somebody had mentioned breakfast – and six or seven boys and girls had appeared, showing signs of recovery. The ingenue who played the Fairy Godmother, still in her crumpled party frock, had offered to see what she could rustle up, reappearing like a true magician with a pot of coffee and a trayload of kidneys on toast which we'd fallen upon like wolves.

Mike Ford and I were still praising this Fairy Godmother as we cleared up after the gang had left.

Robina had then beckoned to me to follow her out into the garden. Puzzled, I'd followed her to the dustbin; she'd lifted the lid and pointed.

There, in all their glory, were six empty catfood tins. I nearly threw up on the spot.

4

Mastering the Irish Whip

Michael Gabbert and I were always keen to recruit new blood – young enterprising reporters ready to join our gang. We found two from my old paper, the *Echo* – one was a keen young lady who had been one of my students on the journalism course at Eastleigh Technical College where I'd done some teaching. She came up with some stories for us, later became a stringer for *The People* and in due course won the Reporter of the Year title.

The second was a young pal from the *Echo* – Rosie – whose family was well connected both with the English Bar and Russian royalty. One Saturday I was working at the subs' desk when Stafford approached, a wicked gleam in his eye.

"Mr Bull," he said. "I found a pretty young blonde on the landing looking for you. She said she couldn't stop, but would I mind bringing your lunch in."

Grins all round from the assembled journos – panic setting in for me. The wicked old sod went on:

"I explained that it was part of my duty to see that younger members of the staff were well looked after and I took her bag of Danish pastries to deliver to you. There were six – but I thought you wouldn't object to one for the delivery boy" and he handed over my gift from Rosie.

The only way I could see to get out of this corner was sharing the pastries with the subs and hoping Stafford choked on his.

Later, one Saturday evening, Rosie dropped in to discuss a story she'd found which she was hoping to sell to the *NoW*. After our chat she left, only to nip back seconds later:

"The cops have towed my Mini away," she said. Apparently she'd left it outside the building – on a Saturday night with dozens of big trucks jockeying for parking slots, delivering huge rolls of newsprint or taking away huge bundles of newspapers. I had forgotten to warn her about this. So I phoned our friends at Snow Hill nick.

"Yes mate," the desk sergeant said. "We always do tow anything parked in Bouverie Street Saturday night. Like you asked us to."

"Well, you might want to take another look at this one," I told him. "The owner is the granddaughter of one of our high court judges."

The sergeant sighed.

"Give us 20 minutes or so and she can pick it up from your front door," he said. And she did.

A little later I had another car problem with our boys in blue.

Stafford, our revered editor, opened his garage door one morning and found it empty. He told Michael Gabbert – and Gabbert told me.

So I called Snow Hill and the duty sergeant wrote down a full description of the editor's Daimler and assured me: "If it's still in London you'll have it back this week at the latest."

Nothing happened that week. Or the next.

In the third week Stafford was stamping about his office – had I been heavy enough with the coppers? Had they been made to understand how important this was?

He was ready to dictate a strong leader complaining that nowhere in London could be safe if bandits could steal people's property with impunity. Were the police asleep at their desks? Where was his car?

All I could do was play for time and keep out of his way. Until Friday ...

"Come and have a drink," he said leading me to the Falstaff. "My neighbour just got back from holiday in Cornwall. Damned funny thing. He opened his garage ... and there was my car! Damned funny – these joy riders have a great sense of humour."

Luckily so did the boys at Snow Hill. A large donation, from my expenses, went to their favourite charity ... an address in Scotland, near a distillery, as I recall.

Apart from the wonders of the courts, sub-editing had its tedious side – the gardening column, the letters page (anyone on the staff could write a letter under a pseudonym incidentally and if printed get a handsome £2 handout.)

Then there was *The Stars Foretell* – horoscopes for the week under the reader's star sign. In the face of all reality, it was extremely popular, despite the fact that each reader would inevitably share the same future for a week as millions of others, along with that week's 'Lucky Day'. The feature was usually placed down-page in two columns. As the months moved on, they shifted up and down the columns .... and, of course the 12 horoscopes varied in length. To make it all fit, the sub had two choices: to carefully rewrite some of the lines to level the columns, or the cheat's way – just to shift the predictions around, regardless of star sign, for a better fit.

So an Aries reader, say, could wind up with Leo's fate instead.

One of our subs even made arbitrary changes to the Lucky Day as a coded message to his girlfriend as to the best day to meet. The editor got wind of this and told him to cut it out.

"But Stafford," he said. "Who knows – this could be the hand of fate guiding my pen."

Being Michael Gabbert's assistant gave me a break from subbing. Now and again I would be hauled off the table to deal with some element of the features/ investigations department. This usually meant re-writing raw copy from Gabbert's investigators, Trevor Kempson and freelance Simon Regan, the latter being a young hippy reporter I'd worked with when Gabbert and I had briefly run a news agency together in Hampshire (it says it all that when he came for interview at 16 he'd produced a tattered passport, with worn pages dropping out and the word 'INTERDIT' stamped in by several border agencies).

One of our most successful 'crusades' was an exposure of a series of popular wrestling tournaments which took place all over the country – and which we suspected were phoney. It was more like a travelling show, with players in the ring using well-rehearsed moves and throws, working from a script. A set tour might start at Bath, move to Cardiff, then to the Isle of Man and back, say, to Blackpool, with five or six bouts on the same programme. It was extremely popular and the shows were often a sell-out. It was no doubt very entertaining, if a trifle less than real.

Now Gabbert and the other members of the team were well used to the routine, having covered lots of these shows in the good old days of the Pompey mafia. We all knew that it was a fix. So Gabbert sent his boys out to cover a series of programmes in different venues. Each time a different reporter was planted in the audience to keep a careful, timed note of the various moves and scenes.

When we sat down to compare them and it was just like the script for a play.

We ran the story over a couple of weeks with the moves and the timings carefully noted for each bout. We also exposed some of the throws as being sheer showmanship, with one of the pair taking a dive. A very popular move was dubbed the Irish Whip, where the champ grabs his opponent and with a flick of the wrist hurls him across the ring onto the ropes.

We'd exposed the racket on Sunday and on the following Wednesday, Gabbert called me into his den. A heavily built, battered heavyweight sat in the visitor's chair.

"John, meet Mr Roberts, alias The Masked Mauler, one of Britain's top wrestlers," he said. "His boss has complained that his shows are all legit and he's sent Mr Roberts to put us right."

The Mauler growled a greeting at me; at the time I turned the scales at not much more than eleven stone.

"OK," said Gabbert. "Can you give my colleague here a taste of, say, the Irish Whip?"

I moved towards the Mauler, who stood up and grabbed my left wrist in his huge paw. I jigged my arm up and down a bit as the Mauler tried to get a better grip … and then I swivelled round and catapaulted him backwards across the room. Unfortunately he knocked his nose on a cupboard and blood spurted out.

I handed him a handkerchief while Gabbert got busy with the first-aid box. To salve the Mauler's blushes, Gabbert's secretary Milly handed him a cheque for £50 as he left.

Over our lunchtime drink, I said to Gabbert: "You remembered, then?" – recalling an incident from our cub reporter days.

"Yes, you threw me down a flight of stairs as I remember. You must have caught me off balance. Judo, wasn't it?"

"Well, it certainly wasn't the Irish Whip, mate. It was Judo then, later enhanced by an unarmed combat course in the RAF during my National Service."

As I fitted in, I was gradually given different jobs to do as Stafford used Gabbert and me as part of his renewal of the wider editorial department – cutting out some of the deadwood, as he put it.

Stafford decided to give me a chance on the 'back bench', the place for whoever was in charge of getting the paper out. My role would be that of copytaster – this meant keeping an eye on all copy that came in live, whether from our own reporters, from the news agencies – the domestic agencies like the Press Association and Extel in the UK – from our own correspondents abroad, or through the international agencies such as Reuters, Associated Press, BUP, or the International News Service.

Gabbert had pointed out to Stafford that at the Associated Press, the American news agency, I'd been handling stories from all over the globe and picking out the best for British newspapers. So I was given a six-month trial.

Eighteen years later I was still doing the job.

The day I started, Stafford gave me some advice:

"I was copytaster here for some years," he said. "If a story came in I wasn't sure about, I'd stick it not on the spike but in my pocket. If it turned out later to be a real story, I'd whip the copy out and pass it over."

And there again I was very lucky. There were a couple of times when the *NoW* missed a good story – but fortunately for me on those couple of occasions, I was either on holiday, or doing some other job for the paper.

One Saturday in July 1969 I was out of the office and didn't take over the copytasting until the 6pm changeover. On a quick leaf through the vast pile of copy in the reject tray (where stories were put before they were consigned to the spike) I kept noticing bits and pieces from Associated Press reporting from somewhere called 'Chukkaduck' or something. There were several sheets of copy carrying the Chukka-whatever dateline.

The story seemed to be about a car running into a river and a girl being drowned. I was intrigued by this agency copy from the US, but with no real clue as to what it was about or why it might be important.

I put in a quick call to the AP and asked the duty copy editor: "Hey pal, what's going down on this Chappaquiddick story?" To which I got the answer: "Looks like Senator Teddy Kennedy is going down, pal."

The senator had been at a Democrat party with politicos and afterwards drove off with one of the girl assistants, Mary Jo Kopechne, in his car. At Chappaquiddick Island they crashed off a bridge into the water; he escaped and swam to safety, but the girl drowned. Kennedy didn't report the accident until the next day, thus casting a shadow that tarnished the rest of his political career.

A front-page story as ever was.

With all the casual subs and reporters joining us on Saturdays, there was a different atmosphere in the constant ringing of phones on the news desk and sports desk. The whole place became as busy as an Arab souk; the casuals put an extra sparkle in the air and our Saturday routine at the *NoW* included a gamble on the horses. Anyone who thought they had a surefire winner was encouraged to pick out a 'winning' nag and we'd all share the bet and the winnings. We were also very fond of Yankees – picking four horses, giving a combination of 11 bets.

As a newcomer I was, of course, given the job of collecting the money. I rather took to the job of collecting the cash – because it also meant I went round paying out the winnings when we had any.

One fine Saturday we had a winning bet, giving a 4-1 return. I recall going round the room offering our punters: "Fivers for all! Get your winning fiver from Honest John! He always pays ..."

Indeed a memory to treasure. See, the thing is that everybody remembers the winners, never the losers.

Of course all the Sunday papers had this same influx of extra professional help on a Saturday. Everyone looked forward to gossip in their break hour and there was a chance to hear the latest – or funniest – incidents at the *Mail*, or *Express*, or the *Mirror*.

It had its hazards, though. I recall having had a drink one evening with an old pal of mine from my *Daily Mirror* days. He may have been a bit careless about the number of whiskies taken, because after a while the chief sub noticed that Charlie had nodded off. Someone gave him a nudge. Somewhat sheepishly he gathered his wits and reality set in: he was in the wrong place. Charlie was supposed to be working the Saturday shift at *The People* – indeed he'd started his day there. We quietly put him in a taxi and sent him home.

5

Over the Wall

Stafford was still finding me new jobs to do, something that annoyed, of course, a whole lot of people, but at the end of the day I was earning my pay. One of the first chores was reading the new books that publishers sent in for review. Most of them were plain awful, but when I found a good one I'd show it to Stafford – the idea was that we could pick out the juicy bits and run it just like any other story.

My first choice was Bryan Bevan's biography of Nell Gwynn featuring the lowdown on King Charles II and the Secret Funds which the wily Charles spent lavishly on the pin-ups of the age, such as Sweet Nell of Old Drury. You know, the one with the juiciest oranges.

My story began: 'One spring the English Secret Service fund paid out £2,500 (an enormous sum in those days) on a very delicate mission. Namely organising visits up the back stairs to the Royal Bedchamber by a wench called Nell Gwynn.'

Another classic was a real blockbuster: *Picasso and his Women* by Jean-Paul Crespelle claimed to be the first biography of Pablo Picasso. Here I really let my hair down and my imagination run wild with vivid descriptions of Pablo's colourful love life. It was a landmark effort, and it added a bit of spice to my reputation. I also hope it sold a lot of books.

Stafford also began to give me reporting assignments. I remember showing up at a Chelsea apartment to interview a chap who claimed to have been a spy (it was never made clear who for – and probably meant he was a double, or even multiple agent, working for everyone). The first thing I noticed

THE GREAT LOVES OF PABLO

By JOHN BULL

IN a Spanish nightclub, a young artist, scarcely more than a boy, sat with his dark eyes fixed on the star of the show, the beautiful Chelito.

As she whirled her body, undressing tantalisingly to the sensual gipsy music, the young man became excited.

He hurried back to his studio and frenziedly covered sheet after sheet of paper with drawings of the girl, naked, in a variety of uninhibited postures.

That was the first linking of the art of Pablo Picasso and his long, legendary private life. A life in which great genius was blended with passionate loves as richly as paints on a palette.

And according to a new book* by Jean-Paul Crespelle, French art critic, as Pablo's mistresses each had a style and beauty of her own, so each inspired a different style of art from Picasso.

Storm

The first mistress was Fernande Olivier, a passively sensual creature, a model in days when it was taken for granted that the girls lay with the painters as well as sitting for them.

She and Picasso literally

OLGA THE DANCER
Knew little of love

Picasso's elegant pictures of the ballet, and after Olga became a mother, the giant matrons with monstrous breasts that he painted between the wars.

In 1931 he fell madly in love with Marie-Therese Walter, a blonde athlete he picked up in the street.

Her sweet influence banished the monsters from his canvasses, replacing them with the sweeping curves of nudes and the flowing lines of his sculpture.

When he first met lovely

A new take on book reviews

43

about him was the quiet hum of a wire-tap machine running out of sight behind the sofa I was sitting on.

The downside of this change of work meant that I was expected to join Stafford in his drinking bouts. Most of the staff fell into this trap from time to time. Friday night was always dangerous. I was lucky to get out of the pub before it closed and I usually had to spend the night at Gabbert's penthouse flat he'd had built off Piccadilly.

Even worse were the times when I was the duty late man. After most people had left there'd be three or four of us, maybe the circulation manager, or one of the production team, or one of the reporters. We were all assembled in Stafford's office for the real drinking – of champagne – to celebrate our survival for another week. Stafford had a nice little fridge in the corner, and now and again, as the newcomer, I was expected to take another bottle out and put it ready in the ice bucket.

One by one the others sloped off and I was left with my editor, now crawling around on the floor.

"Come and help me," he drawled. "I've dropped my glasses." Naturally I obliged and joined him on all fours – too tactful to remind him he was still wearing his specs.

Eventually the call came from the night watchman. Used to the drill, he'd called a cab to take the editor home. I joined him in the cab to make sure he was delivered to the right address.

I helped him to the front door, both of us (as in a seaside postcard) putting a finger to our lips and saying 'shusshh, shusshh – mushn't wake the wife.' I made sure he was safely inside and then I got back in the cab to get to Piccadilly.

The following Wednesday I met Stafford walking down Bouverie Street, as I walked up from the river. We met at the front door.

"It was you who saw me home on Saturday, right?"

I nodded.

"Well p'raps we should have wakened my wife. When she came down to let her lunch guests in, she found me asleep on the doormat."

We walked into the building together – giggling like a couple of truant kids.

I was still reviewing any new book that would suit the *NoW* readers – one of the best was *The Springing of George Blake* by Sean Bourke, its author being a prime example of the colourful Wormwood Scrubs old boy.

The black sheep of a large Limerick family which included an actor and a poet, Bourke was handed seven years for attempted murder of a detective in the Met. The parcel bomb hadn't gone off. Oh, and he became editor of the Scrubs prison magazine *New Horizon* (well it's a better banner than, say *Over the Wall*). Sean befriended fellow inmate George Blake – then regarded by MI6 as 'the most dangerous double-agent in history'. He had been taken prisoner during the Korean War and turned by the communist forces to spy for Russia. Back in Britain, in a secret trial, he was found guilty of warning the Russians about a plan to build an 'eavesdropping' tunnel under the Soviet Embassy in Berlin.

The maximum penalty for breaking the Official Secrets Act was then 14 years, but the judge multiplied it by three to make it a round 42. And Blake was banged up in the Scrubs.

As if all that wasn't bizarre enough – and let's face it, in the so-called Cold War, both sides came up with outlandish ideas that would have fitted neatly into a script for the Goons or Monty Python, never mind James Bond – Blake's escape from jail five years later left any sense of reality far, far behind.

Fleet Street and the BBC had a feeding-frenzy on the assumption that the ruthless KGB were the masterminds behind the breakout. The truth was a little less glamorous. The minds behind this snatch were those of Sean Bourke and two militant anti-nuclear bomb protesters, Pat Pottle and Michael Randle, who also did time in the Scrubs. They too befriended Blake, on the grounds that his sentence was political and inhumane.

Just as the *NoW*'s first edition was rolling off the presses on Saturday October 22, 1966, Blake was wriggling his way between the bars of his cell in the Scrubs, and fumbling up a rope ladder made of knitting needles dangling down the wall of the jail. From the wall he jumped down onto the roof of a tall removal van, breaking an arm in the process.

The best bits of the escape didn't emerge until years later – according to Nick Cohen in an obituary of Pottle in *The New Statesman* headlined 'A jailbreak out of an Ealing comedy' (October 9, 2000), Pottle and Randle had asked a friend, a well-to-do lady, if they could stay in her cellar for a few days while she was away. She returned early and innocently asked who else was in the cellar.

"George Blake?" she shrieked in sheer disbelief. "*The* George Blake – the most wanted man in Britain ...?"

Then she had an attack of hysteria and confessed all to her doctor.

Meanwhile Blake was driven across France in the secret compartment of a camper van; he and Bourke travelled across Europe to the safety of communist East Germany and the amazement of the Stasi secret police guarding the border checkpoint.

Bourke's book told the story of his two-year stay as a guest of the KGB in Moscow. He claimed he was in fear of his life all the time and even suggested that Blake had been ordered to kill him. He finally managed to return to Ireland, where he died penniless some years later.

And what of George Blake? You may well ask. Imagine my surprise, one morning in November 2012, when I opened the *Daily Mail* to see a photo of a very distinguished gentleman celebrating his 90th birthday at a dacha country house near Moscow. None other than Mr Blake himself – or to give him his Russian title, Lieutenant-Colonel KGB retd.

He was quoted as telling journalists "I am spending the happiest years of my life in Vladimir Putin's Russia."
Questioned about his famous jailbreak, he pointed to his stiff right arm, broken in the leap from the prison wall. Apparently he now lives in a quiet Moscow suburb with his wife Ida on a state pension, and enjoys visits from his three British sons. Well I'm glad it all ended so well ...

6

The Battle for the Soul of the News of the World

We didn't know it, but everything was about to change at the *NoW* – and this is how I imagine it all began ...

Picture a delightful morning in autumn, when Paris wears her prettiest dresses, the glowing tints of chestnut trees, of red and gold, the streets full of parading demoiselles, lovers and dreamers, music from street singers filling *les boulevards* ...

In his spacious apartment with its wonderful views of the City of Light, Professor Derek Jackson is rubbing the sleep from his eyes, preparing to welcome the new day.

Then he remembers he is selling his 25 percent family holding in *News of the World* shares; lately the income from this share has been – to put it politely – not what it had been.

He ponders:

"How much could I get for my shares on the open market?"

And the answer comes in the rotund shape of Mr Robert Maxwell, a print and publications predator. With the grin of the hunter around his hungry jaw, he announces that he has offered a mighty £26 million in a takeover bid for the *News of the World*.

So, as the autumn of 1968 turns to winter, began the Battle for the Soul of the world's biggest-selling title – and the staff of the paper feared they were facing a bleak future.

Stafford Somerfield instructed me to write a draft leader for Sunday's paper, the first of the New Year: it would be an appeal to English loyalties – a way of 'wrapping' the paper in the Union Jack. With my name, why wouldn't I?

'We're as English as Roast Beef and Yorkshire pudding,' we said – and so on, for our millions of readers. The BBC rallied to the flag but (much to the delight of our competitors) reality pointed to Maxwell winning the war.

"There's just one way out," said the Carr faction. "We'll have to sell a slice to another rich bugger, someone we can trust to see things our way."

They came up with a virtually unknown Aussie, an ex-Oxford man (where he is said to have displayed left-wing leanings and joined the Labour Party), son of a chap who owned a group of newspapers Down Under, a set-up regarded (wrongly) as run by backwoodsmen compared with the sophistication of London and Fleet Street.

"Well he's our man," said the *NoW* owners, workers and supporters. "We can't go wrong – the man's got money and some reputation in the financial world and we can certainly keep him well under control. After all he's just a simple sheep-shearer."

When I think with hindsight of all the sheepish media tycoons owning newspapers and TV stations worldwide who have wound up being being shorn by Rupert Murdoch since that fateful day in January 1969... it's (as we often say in the business) truly a story you couldn't make up.

In his book *Rupert Murdoch – A Business Biography*, my one-time apprentice reporter Simon Regan has a racy account of the battle for the *Screws*. He pictures Robert Maxwell as a power-driven financial manipulator, rich and clever enough to get the best wheeler-dealers in the City of London on his side; and Sir William Carr and the rest of his family and longtime shareholders in an uneasy alliance with Rupert Murdoch – an unknown in the City.

In this big-time contest, seen as the Champ Robert v the Novice Rupert, the outcome was regarded as a foregone conclusion: Maxwell was pictured on the TV news, off to the last most important meeting of the money men, grinning complacently, lips curling with anticipation. The Carr-Murdoch alliance was regarded as a touch-and-go, long-odds bet. But on the fateful day the meeting hall was packed with a new mob of shareholders. The Carrs took the unprecedented move of agreeing to give shares to numbers of journalists and others on the staff of the *NoW* in an attempt to block the sale to Maxwell. They just had to give the shares back later ...

When the dust of battle cleared, Rupert emerged as the winner. He'd got his first Fleet Street newspaper. Maxwell, the loser, huffed and turned his back. He told the BBC cameras that Murdoch had used 'the law of the jungle' to win.

Rupert smiled sympathetically and shrugged ("just the luck of the game").

Meanwhile we, the workers, were down on our knees, thanking the Almighty for our salvation.

Our new boss, Rupert, was an enigma to Stafford and his supporters, including Michael Gabbert and me.

He made little impact at first. In fact considering his reputation, he adopted a remarkably low profile. It was uncannily as if we had a mouse somewhere in the house that we couldn't find.

Early on we had a private party for some of the editorial staff – a retiring do for Joan, Stafford's super-efficient and angelic secretary.

As he often did, Stafford put me in charge of keeping the glasses topped up, at a table in the Big Room alongside the record player, where the new Australian boss (a few years older than me) happily took over the chore of changing the music.

It probably occurred to most of us then that we would soon be dancing to his tune; it certainly crossed my mind.

It fitted his general approach to the office – a quiet, easy-going presence. We knew so little about him that any slight rumour whistled through the ranks disseminating wild and eccentric info ....

"Rupert hates suede shoes, y'know. Yes, can't stand men in suede shoes – been known to sack people there and then if they showed up wearing 'em to the office. S' a fact!"

"He's terribly mean, Rupert. Yeah, won't spend a penny more than he can help. Look at his shabby suits ... that tells you a lot about the man."

And this one, which I heard from several *NoW* executives at different times:

"Murdoch – he's mean all right. I was walking down Fleet Street with him when I noticed that the sole of one of his shoes was flapping loose. It made this awful flip-flap noise all the way down the road. I couldn't stand the damned racket and I kept fretting that we'd bump into someone like Rees Mogg, or Bernard Levin, and we'd wind up as a diary item in The Times or, God forbid, the Daily Express.

"So I suggested we pop into the men's footwear specialists in the Strand to fix him up with a new pair of shoes. He was having none of it. And after lunch at the Savoy we still had to put up with the slip-slap from his shoe all the way back to Bouverie Street."

The first of Rupert's changes was hardly important in the scale of great events – but it did send shockwaves through the ranks of the scribes and inkies. At the start of our working week we were told that the six-column format of the broadsheet pages of the great *News of the World* was in future going to be seven columns. For some it was a cause for a loud wailing and gnashing of teeth and breast-beating. It produced an thunderous outcry such as Londoners might have raised if authority tried to change the numbers on the face of Big Ben from Roman numerals to Arabic. After all, the layout men had been doing the six-column version for years and could do it with their eyes closed, so weren't keen on changing; and the new seven-column layout would cram in more stories, giving the compositors even more to do.

In order to fit the new layout, the type size of the text throughout would shrink from eight point down to seven point – just about enough to give us another column on the page. Quite how our new managing director managed to get that past our very militant inkies – the guys who would have to do the setting of the new type format – I never discovered. But I'm pretty sure that money must have dropped chinking into the pockets of the composing-room boys.

We editorial types feared that this would mean a serious change in the grand flagship Sunday paper with its longtime proud boast:

ALL HUMAN LIFE IS THERE

The look of the old paper changed overnight and Gabbert and I couldn't decide whether Rupert judged it would seem a bigger bargain to the reader – or was just designed to demonstrate to us who was really running the show.

The Letters Page editor – David Gordois – was warned to look out for piles of complaints from 'Disgusted of Clapham Junction' and 'ex-Reader of Wallsend-on-Tyne.' Stafford decided to put a bold face on it by saying that since most of the readers were over 50 and their eyes were not as sharp as they once were, it might just go unnoticed.

But then Stafford was no great friend of the readers' page – I think he resented the fact that readers didn't always agree with him. For instance, one time when I was sitting in for the letters editor I found a gem from the widow of one of the shadowy figures of the British justice system – a 'deputy' hangman.

Her letter ran to several pages – but the gist of it was that her husband had been chosen to despatch a notorious killer. Hubby had gone through the ritual of meeting his man before the event, as was apparently the custom.

Her husband, she said, had been struck by the prisoner's dazzling smile – and had congratulated the condemned man on his perfect teeth.

"They're false, of course," the condemned man had said. "Made for me by a dental surgeon who I helped after he had been released from the horrors of a concentration camp during the war. Look here, you're wearing dentures – try these on for size and if they fit you can have them ... when I've gone."

'They fitted perfectly,' the woman said in her letter. 'It's an unusual story isn't it?'

Well, of course I made it the prize letter of the week and duly sent the widow a cheque.

Stafford was not best pleased when he saw it – apparently he'd banned any mention of false teeth from the paper. And I have to admit that I've been known to have nightmares when I think of that poor woman. Can you imagine? Night after night, the last thing she saw as hubby turned out the light was those gleaming murderer's choppers grinning at her from a glass of water by the bed.

This rather strange year of 1968 suddenly turned septic with the horrific kidnappping of 55-year-old Muriel McKay, wife of the deputy chairman of the *NoW*, Alick McKay.

At this time Rupert had flown off to Australia, to look after his newspaper empire down under. He suggested to his trusted deputy that he was welcome to use his Rolls Royce while he was away. Alick wasn't particularly interested, but Muriel was entranced by the car, so she was allowed to use it whenever she wanted.

Tragically, a few days after Christmas, she disappeared. And it wasn't long before the *News of the World* received a ransom demand.

At that awful time there was a sort of bewildered air around the paper – I remember one of the crime reporters musing over a pint: "You know, John, I can't recall a kidnapping in England – ever. Seems to me a peculiarly un-British thing to do."

We knew what he meant.

That one sentence probably tells you more about the heart

of the *News of the World* than any amount of media comment and Fleet Street lore. To the *NoW* reader, England was the land of roast beef and Yorkshire pud; it was jewel thefts in country mansions, train robberies, or serial murders of women in dark and narrow city streets. Or shady dealings of espionage, involving shifty foreigners.

The kidnappers had mistaken Muriel for Rupert's wife Anna and demanded a million-pound ransom for her return. Half-a-dozen 'drop' arrangements for the cash were made by Scotland Yard, but no-one ever showed up. After five weeks and many phone conversations, the kidnappers were traced to an isolated farm in Hertfordshire.

In October 1970 Arthur Hosein, a 34-year-old former squaddie, and his younger brother Nizamodeen – originally from Trinidad – were found guilty of murder (one of the very first cases of a murder conviction without a body) and jailed for life.

Muriel's body was never found.

7

Being John Field

The days really brightened for me in 1969 when I was given a weekly column in the *NoW.*

The timing couldn't have been better for me if I'd planned it. In fact I owed it all to the 'star' of the Profumo scandal of 1963 – Christine Keeler.

The Profumo story had everything – sexy call girls, a shadowy osteopath (Stephen Ward, whose sideline was introducing good-time girls to prominent men, sometimes at exclusive parties at the country mansion of a peer of the realm, Lord Astor), a Soviet naval officer who was a suspected spy from the Soviet Embassy, and John Profumo, the Minister for War.

Profumo finally admitted he'd lied to the Commons in saying he never had a sexual relationship with Christine Keeler. He duly resigned and the scandal was held to be partly responsible for the later fall of the Macmillan government.

Six years on, Christine Keller had written her memoirs and was looking to sell them. Rupert immediately jumped in with a bid that no one would match – the figure bandied about the office was £25,000.

He won the auction for this apparently red-hot stuff and was determined to serialise the whole story in the *NoW.* This caused a feeding frenzy in the media with all the bosses who lost out in the auction immediately denouncing Rupert as the 'Dirty Digger' accusing him of making money from muck-raking (presumably out of sour grapes because they'd missed out being able to do a bit of muck-raking of their own).

David Dimbleby wanted Rupert to appear on his influential

TV show where he gave prominent figures a grilling. Stafford and Michael Gabbert advised him against it, because they feared that it would turn into an inquisition – they suggested someone more TV-savvy instead: themselves. But Rupert was determined.

The programme (you can still watch it on YouTube) begins with a bitchy and envious comment from the newspaper Establishment, in the shape of Canadian press magnate Roy Thompson, owner of *The Times* and *The Sunday Times*, followed by a sneer or two from Robert Maxwell.

Then the camera goes into Stafford's spacious office to show him in conference with Rupert and the senior news staff, Charlie Markus and Frank Butler, discussing the treatment and presentation of the Keeler memoirs.

Dimbleby next gives Rupert a grilling to camera, to which Rupert responds genially, and comes across as a defender of the ordinary man's right to know what's going on. Why should the English Establishment be protected from exposure? Why shouldn't people be able to read what the rich and powerful get up to?

Dimbleby makes the point that it is unfair to Profumo to rake it all up again but Rupert praises Profumo for re-habilitating himself. "We can forgive – but we shouldn't forget," he says.

David Dimbleby turns to Mrs Anna Murdoch, who gently defends her husband.

"He likes to go into newsagents and shuffle the papers around to make the *NoW* more prominent," she says with a saucy grin to the camera.

When he gets a bit tougher and asks if she is ashamed of the paper she neatly puts him down: "No, I'm proud of it – and *that* was a very pretentious thing to say."

A neat slapdown for young Dimblepops.

Was Christine Keeler's memoir just a sleazy lowlife story? Actually there was nothing much that was shockingly new in her story of sexy doings at the top of the political tree.

When the Profumo scandal had broken in the early 60s it had been instantly and enthusiastically taken up by David Frost's satirical TV show *That Was the Week That Was*, with its ground-breaking ridicule of the Establishment and the political elite. In Europe and the United States over the decades since, there have been many movies based on the Profumo-Keeler story, as well as songs and musical stage shows, including Andrew Lloyd Webber's *Stephen Ward*. The adventures of Christine Keeler and her pal Mandy Rice Davies continue to capture the public imagination: it was Rice Davies who added a now-famous and oft-quoted line to the English language: "Well he would say that wouldn't he?" referring to a courtroom denial by Lord Astor that he had ever had sex with her.

Every now and then someone picks over the bones of that quote. In January 2013 there was an interesting exchange in the letters page of *The Times*. Top-drawer legal eagle Sir Ivan Lawrence wrote that he had been in court for the committal proceedings of Stephen Ward: at the time, he was junior to Ward's defence counsel James Burge. He wrote:

> *What she actually said was 'of course it's not untrue that I have had relations with Lord Astor. I'm not going to perjure myself in court.' ... I have before me as I write, the precise note. With all my imperfections, I could hardly have avoided recording such a significant and witty statement had it been uttered.*

Mandy quickly replied in *The Times*:

> *I too was present at Stephen Ward's hearing at Marylebone Magistrates Court in June 1963 and most certainly did say: "Well he would, wouldn't he?" It was said in reply to Mervyn Griffith-Jones (prosecution) when it was put to me that Lord Astor had denied any sexual allegations in regard to myself. The palest ink is not always better than the best of memory, Sir Ivan – besides I have before me the court transcript."*

My column – called 'One Point of View' – first saw the light of print on the Sunday we started running Christine Keeler's story, in October 1969. Everyone was talking about it, so I ran a mock-innocent heading on my column: 'WHO did you say she was?'

What a week to start a new column. There's only one thing being talked about. WHO did you say she was?

ONE POINT OF VIEW

By John Field

THE British Fleet has sunk to a mere handful of ships. Mourners include Earl Mountbatten, once the great Supremo, and Mr Raymond Blackman, editor of *Jane's Fighting Ships.* He thought the Royal Navy should go Dutch with the Netherlands fleet to make up a viable force.

Then a ship called the Admiral Nelson, carrying a cargo of fertiliser, hurled herself aground off the Norfolk coast. *Out of shame?*

☆

LET no one stop the hippies from buying that remote island off

high window. "I've nothing left to live for," he said before he died. Harold was 81. His girl lived at the same old people's home in the Isle of Wight. *Neither the joy, nor the pain of love is the exclusive property of the young.*

☆

WE'RE a nation of dog lovers, they say. Two policemen were fined for letting alsatians Flash and Fury die from heat stroke in a mini-van on a hot day. They were stupid men. But a couple on TV's *Opportunity Knocks* show made a dog he'd a flaming brand in his jaws. Presumably to demonstrate some kind of talent. *That's something we can do without.*

was longer than the first. *It's simpler to pay by cheque*

☆

RICHARD CROSSMAN, the Social Services Minister, wrote it in this paper and said it again in Yorkshire this week. There are 4,000 children in hospitals who should not be there. *Mr Crossman is right to speak up. But let's actually do something and get the poor kids out*

☆

WHAT about the four-day outing to Torquay which 1,000 publicans and drinks trade people will be starting tomorrow? On the programme are four wine and spirit tastings, four wine and spirit re-

The first John Field column

Stafford had vetoed calling it the John Bull column – "Everyone will think it's a made-up name," he said. So we had settled on 'John' for me and 'Field' for the second half of Stafford's surname. I'd still continue to use my real name on features and book reviews.

John Field seemed to go down well with readers from the start as the crisp, short pieces and the punchlines took effect. The tagline the paper used from time to time was 'the column that takes a common-sense look at life'.

THEY THINK WE'RE ALL SUCKERS !

One Point of View

WE REALLY do stand for the three-car trick in this country. In the past fortnight I have twice travelled from London to Bristol and back in a day (YOUR Inter-City they call it.)

The buffet was open on only one of the four trains, two trains were late and on one journey nobody bothered to check or collect my ticket.

There were no day return tickets, of course; you can't get them unless you start out so late in the morning that it's not practical to go there and back the same day.

Last week I decided to keep a check on the wonders of STD telephones.

Of 54 calls I made from my office, 12 were

Keeping the trains on their toes

58

For several weeks Stafford kept up the idea that he was going to take the column over – but as the mailbag of readers letters began to get heavier, he dropped the idea and left it to me. He also started to ask me more often to have a go at the leader column.

He took me aside and suggested I put in an expenses sheet – handy extra pocket-money in those days. He also arranged for the company to pay my membership fee at the Press Club and my annual membership of Hampshire Cricket Club. And I'm happy to say I had recently been given my first rise in pay (a comfortable extra £800 a year).

"After all," he explained, "you're an asset to the paper ... you're the *News of the World*'s figleaf!" He probably said much the same thing to Noyes Thomas and some of the others: by doing book reviews, and hiding some of the sexy stuff, we added a bit of 'tone' to the paper.

Of course my rivals on the design and make-up staff were dismissive of the column.

"It reads like a music-hall act with all these punchlines," one said. And so it did – but, then again, why not? I had pinched the idea from my boyhood idols of the old-fashioned music hall and adapted it to make cynical comments on politics and current affairs.

After all, the *News Of* was actually chasing the same audience. Here's one of the punchlines from my first column:

A 19-year-old chap in Keyworth, Notts, was fined £5 in the magistrates court for posing as a policeman and trying to arrest a cyclist. The rider took a long look at the young man in his smart blue uniform and saw through him straight away. He just happened to be wearing brown boots.
        Brown boots, I ask you.

Now they don't come much more old-fashioned than that – *Brahn Boots* was a monologue poem about a Cockney funeral by Weston and Lee, often performed by comedian Stanley Holloway.

John Field lasted well into the 1970s ... a record for any *News of the World* column.

At one Friday evening editorial conference – in the Falstaff, of course – Stafford got into a 'discussion' with some of our female freelances. He was advocating the paper run an attack on the Women's Lib movement that was getting a lot of publicity on TV and the newspapers – especially the bits involving bra-burning. Bizarrely, what had really riled him was the existence of a Ladies Waiting Room at Waterloo station. It was an insult that men should be barred from the room! Since my wife Robina was a supporter of the formidable women's movement in Southampton along with other Amazons – like the politically minded Jill Kushlick and her chum Jan Griffiths – I went on quietly sipping my beer.

With a full head-of-steam, Stafford was running through suggestions to hit back at these dominatrices (his word) and one idea that he seized upon was a publicity stunt.

"We men, the breadwinners and the freedom fighters of England, must take a stand against this insult to our manhood." He was in full flow, arms waving and in grave danger of spilling his whisky.

And he'd captured the cheers of several males – more beer-swillers than freedom fighters it has to be said. Then he noticed me.

"John," he hollered, putting arm round my shoulder. "You're the very man to go there and challenge this stupid rule. John Bull, standing up for England and St George."

"He'll get arrested," said Hinchcliffe, the lawyer.

One of the freelances protested that women would stop buying the paper.

People, including me, quietly slipped off into the night, with me praying that the idea would quietly vanish.

However, to be on the safe side I stopped shaving, hoping to grow enough of a beard in order to pass unrecognised if the stunt got into the paper. I also had to pretend to be enthusiastic about the idea while keeping out of Stafford's way.

A fortnight went by (and my beard was looking quite respectable) before 'Long Tom', the *NoW*'s lofty snapper, popped his head round the door of our office and asked me to brief him "about this Waterloo stunt tomorrow."

So I found myself outside Waterloo's forbidding entrance to the Ladies Only Waiting Room ... the dragons' den. Tom bought himself a coffee and leaned against a handy pillar.

Deep breath as I pushed open the door and slunk into the room. Several dozen pairs of female eyes swivelled my way and a couple of younger matrons stood up like guardsmen on parade.

"Don't panic, ladies," I said. "Just a routine inspection of the ...." Not a single idea came to me, so I pointed up at the ceiling. At least it made a change to have them stare upwards instead of glaring at me. Talk about a Mexican stand-off.

A sudden shout behind me and a large hand on my shoulder. A blinding flash of light and I found myself blinking at Tom, while a gruff police sergeant said: "All right, sir, just you come along with me. Sorry to disturb you, ladies."

Of course we adjourned to the bar, me blessing Tom for talking the sergeant into helping out.

It made a nice two-column news story at the top of the page under the John Field byline. John Field got the blame (John Bull escaped scot-free thanks to the disguise) and Stafford was right – we got hundreds of letters. Not one from a bloke.

8

Editor Emeritus

At this time Gabbert and I and his freelance crew were riding high. We had helped Stafford get rid of some of the more old-fashioned attitudes on the paper and in line with the changes that Rupert had introduced we were convinced we were chasing a much better circulation figure. We were already claiming a weekly sale of five million, which certainly pleased Rupert. We hadn't yet learned that he was a driven man and there would *never* come a time that he would stop taking over newspapers and news media. Simon Regan made a personal assessment of Murdoch in his book *Rupert Murdoch – A Business Biography*. Regan couldn't spell, couldn't write and could never settle to painstaking work, but he had one clear asset – a sort of brash understanding of people that took him a long way. His assessment was this: that because Murdoch's father died young, his son never had a chance to prove himself – and he would go on trying to impress his lost father for the rest of his life.

Well it is a theory and there are plenty of similar examples in history.

Gabbert was fond of sharing his plans with me. With a comfortable rise in circulation, when the ageing Sir William Carr retired there would be a seat on the board for Stafford, the editor's chair for Gabbert, and a space for me as his deputy. The only way is up, he used to say.

The future certainly looked rosy as we sat sipping drinks with his wife Karen, in the roof garden of his penthouse just off Piccadilly, watching the glorious sunset over Hyde Park. The building of this penthouse was a typical Gabbert saga. With some of his usual fancy footwork he managed to get a lease on the roof of a block of flats one street away from Park Lane. It was a venture in which the whole gang of us played a part; the building work was masterminded by a chap who used to build swimming pools in the Channel Islands – he was a super cook, too.

The roof garden, by the way, was paved with beautiful tiles from the floor of the London Stock Exchange. Gabbert's builder got wind that the Exchange was to be re-floored, put in a bid for the old tiles, and won. He advertised the floor in lots and made enough to get the penthouse share for next to nothing. Shangri-la.

Somehow we overlooked the one basic flaw in our crafty plan for a wonderful future. Stafford took it into his head to try to run things his way – and to ignore the new ideas that Rupert wanted to introduce. He relied on the 'gold-lined' contract that he'd negotiated with the Carrs to keep him safe from the sack. He said it was drawn up for him by Lord Goodman, the leading lawyer of the day – who incidentally had offices in the *NoW* building in Bouverie Street – and was foolproof. And he began to play the dangerous game of going his own sweet way without consulting Rupert.

While Stafford was on holiday in sunnier climes, Rupert took over the editor's job and made some serious changes to the old man's style. When a sidekick phoned him and outlined what was going on, Stafford got the next plane to London and hot-footed it back to Bouverie Street. Cigar in mouth, he set about changing things back again.

It wasn't long before Rupert got tired of this sort of thing and called Stafford in: the interview lasted all of three minutes and Stafford was sacked.

So our dream scene lasted until Thursday February 26, 1970. As the *Evening Standard* screamed:

Stafford had edited the *NoW* for ten years. It was to be the end of an era.

I can picture him now, the shock registering still on his face. But, Stafford-like, he bounced back (maybe thinking of his £100,000 severance pay) and invited the entire editorial staff of the paper to a farewell lunchtime booze-up at the Punch tavern in Fleet Street. Michael Gabbert quickly stepped in:

"You are not going to get drunk because you will certainly be on TV tonight. I will take you to El Vino and we will share a bottle of champagne, and then you go home."

Stafford meekly agreed. It was Gabbert's way of saying thanks for giving us our big chance.

I mistily recall being back at the office later that afternoon, along with the new editor Tiny Lear, and Ron Lawrence, the chief sub, dealing hazily through a miasma of alcohol with the copy piled in Ron's basket from those reporters still capable of ravelling up a story. Actually some of them truly did write clearer English when pissed.

Stafford takes it on the chin

As a commenter on the press once said: "When Murdoch sacks editors he often gives them the title 'Editor Emeritus'. One of them asked what the title actually meant. Murdoch replied: 'It's Latin, Frank – E means you're out, and meritus means you deserve to be out.'"

Stafford's dismissal was the start of Rupert's masterplan to free himself of the Carr family shareholders and to gain full control of the *News of the World.* At this point the Carrs still owned most of the business, but Rupert was gradually buying them out. Firing Stafford, who was regarded as their 'creature', would help show who was in charge.

Over the years, the Carrs had been merrily buying up all kinds of businesses – some of them you might think rather bizarre for a newspaper company. They already owned the famous Berrow's group – originally *Berrow's Journal* – accepted as the first real British newspaper and certainly the first ever to have a woman as editor. Berrows had papers up and down the country. But more oddly, perhaps, they had also acquired several golf clubs, which reminds me of an old music-hall joke:

> *"Rich? I'll say. His father gave him a set of golf clubs for his birthday – Wentworth, St Andrews, etc."*

And if my memory serves, the Carrs also picked up somewhere along the way a plastics factory and a firm specialising in electrical work. They even acquired a paper mill, which actually might have been handy – except that the story on the Street was that the place was allowed to decay. Rupert took one look, shuddered, and sold it virtually for scrap.

From all this he emerged as the sole owner of the *News of the World.* But anyone who imagined he was going to stop there wasn't really following the plot.

The heaviest presence in Fleet Street at that time was the Mirror Group, which was widely regarded as the most successful newspaper business in Britain, and was headed by Cecil King, a renowned newspaper-editor-turned-magnate.

Also contending was the Canadian Roy Thompson, owner of *The Times* and *Sunday Times* – who was also forging ahead by turning his back on noted journalists and relying on educating his own team of young pretenders, rather as that other notable Canadian, later Lord Beaverbrook, did with the *Express* newspapers. In effect Rupert did something similar – except he also tended to poach talented editors and newspaper managers, encouraging them to bring on their own young challengers.

There was a long cat-and-mouse period when Cecil King and his henchman Hugh Cudlipp dithered around trying one thing after another to outgrow the rest of the pack. They took over the old solid Labour party organ the *Daily Herald* owned by trade unions. This paper had flourished in the era of the post-war Labour movement and the Mirror Group bought the paper cheap, renaming it the *Sun* and hoping to turn the broadsheet into a companion paper to the tabloid *Daily Mirror*. The *Daily Herald*, however, lost momentum as things got 'better' for the Brits in the days of plentiful manual work. The workers chased more frivolous stuff – with TV leading the charge.

We working-class lads in Fleet Street couldn't fail to notice that our old mates on the *Mirror*, funded by fat salaries, were now beginning to climb into the middle classes; I personally knew two sub-editors who had bought redundant church rectories near Orpington and joined the local gun club. The paper didn't have much competition – it led the market and so the boys were paid higher salaries than the rest of us.

Both papers were causing headaches and the *Herald* became known to commentators as 'King's Cross'. And then the boardroom had the bright idea that since Murdoch was looking around for acquisitions, they could sell him this pig in a poke – and hope he choked on it. He'd have to buy the title, the building and the presses; it would cost him a small fortune, the *Mirror* would reap the benefits and Murdoch's dream of having a daily would be scuppered.

Oh dear, oh bloody dear, how naive could they get? It makes me want to go back in time, take Cecil and Hugh over to the White Swan, the *Mirror*'s favoured pub, known cynically as 'The Stab in the Back,' and over a couple of pints hammer some sense into their deluded, old-fashioned heads.

Rupert couldn't believe his luck. He walked about the office with a 'cat that got the cream' smile on his face, greeting everyone with his trademark, a pleasant 'G'day.' What we at the heart of the *NoW* knew and what no-one else did, was that Rupert, long haunted by the waste of our printing machines standing idle six days a week (I personally believe it kept him awake at nights) had done what the rest of Fleet Street said was impossible: he had 'persuaded' the great and all-powerful print unions to accept printing a new daily paper on *the same presses* as the *NoW*. Bingo! He could sell off the unwanted *Herald*'s buildings and presses and thus acquire the paper for more-or-less nothing.

In the climate of those years, with unions calling the shots all the time in every dispute and the rich owners always giving in to their demands, this news was 'sensational' to say the least. To me it was an amazing coup and I've always regarded it as a simple case of Rupert acquiring a new daily paper with Cecil King's own money. I wish I'd been able to listen in on the negotiations between these two heavyweights – Murdoch v The Print Unions.

According to Simon Regan's account, the upshot was that Murdoch bought the *Sun* for £50,000 down – about the price of a decent semi in South London at the time – and a further maximum £600,000 a year over six years, to be paid out of profits (presumably if there were any). He would pitch the paper as a direct competitor to the *Mirror*.

Of course there was much speculation about who would edit the new paper, which Murdoch immediately changed from broadsheet to tabloid. Since Stafford's sacking, Gabbert had kept a low profile – he confided in me that, if he had been mooted as editor, it might unleash a wave of anti-Gabbert propaganda. I wasn't sure about that, but I had reason to believe that Gabbert did not want to push himself into the firing line. It was going to be a really tough job, taking on the Mirror Group at their own game.

At the same time, Gabbert had seen another opportunity open up; he had got wind of a large country house for sale

Rupert picks up another bargain

in Surrey, set in spacious grounds, and with its own lake, surrounded by its own woodland. The house was sadly neglected – and hence at a bargain price. He put his Park Lane penthouse on the market, quit the newspaper business, and later boldly announced to me that he'd become the 'lord of the manor.'

His wife Karen was equally delighted to be the lady of the manor, especially since they now had a baby son.

"What are you going to do for money?" was my obvious question.

Breaking the news: John Wayne beats cancer

"Turn it into a country club, of course," he said. And he did.

This left me hanging in mid-air with no-one in the upper echelons to champion my corner. I think my Fleet Street acquaintances expected me to join *The Sun*. But I had no interest in working for a brash daily tabloid – especially since I had sometime earlier crossed swords with Albert 'Larry' Lamb, its new editor in chief who, with Bernard Shrimsley, had moved over from the Mirror Group. Besides, I still had the John Field column, my feature-subbing work, and the copytasting.

Since then the myth has grown that the Murdoch *Sun* was a runaway success. It wasn't. Most people saw it as the *Daily Mirror* with bare tits and things didn't get better when the *Mirror* also went for the Page 3 approach, meaning that the *Sun* wasn't really offering anything different.

Back at the still top-selling *NoW* I arrived early one Saturday morning to find Rupert alone sitting in the copytaster's chair, shuffling through the foreign copy.

Had he taken over my job?

"You look nervous," he said.

"Ah, yes. I suppose I do. Stafford's gone and Gabbert's gone ... and ... well I feel a little vulnerable."

Murdoch stood up, pulled back the chair for me to sit: "Stafford used to refer to you as the *NoW* figleaf with your John Field column and feature stories – and so here you are. Good luck."

From a housekeeping point of view the new tabloid brought great changes to the *NoW*, which was still a broadsheet paper. The *Sun* editorial team moved into the Big Room and our editorial staff moved up a floor – with subs and sports staff sharing a smaller space and Charlie Markus and his reporters in quarters down the corridor.

I did very well out of it, as it happened, since I was moved in with what had been Gabbert's chief investigators, Trevor Kempson and Bill Rankine (an upmarket heavyweight commentator – another 'figleaf') and sharing their secretary Milly, the 'Sauf' London gal.

Our office was at the end of a corridor leading to an interior staircase – and on the other side of that, in what had once been a separate building, was the office of a couple of *Sun* writers – columnist Jon Akass, a sort of apprentice 'Cassandra' (the *Mirror*'s star columnist for many years) with equally acid bite – and none other than my old pal from our early days in Hampshire, John Dodd, once the raw junior cub reporter of the *Hants and Sussex News* in the up-market East Hampshire town favoured by actors, writers and arty folk. Doddy was now the writer of humorous, off-beat pieces for the *Sun*.

One result of them being just along the corridor was the institution of the Wednesday afternoon tea party in their office (for 'tea' read 'champagne') where we swapped ideas and traded gossip.

Some of us weekly columnists used to gather at the Blackfriars, a popular watering hole round the corner from Fleet Street and near the bridge which gave the pub its name. On a sunny Friday lunchtime you'd find me with Doddy and Akass from the *Sun*, sitting on the low wall in front of the boozer, pint in hand; and often the big stars such as Clive James and George Melly from the *Observer* or *Sunday Times*.

Now and again they'd let us lesser folk say something – such as when rumour was rife that Murdoch was about to take over *The Times* and I got a round of applause and a free drink when I revealed the shock-horror rumour that *Rupert had sacked eight people from* The Times *Porcelain column alone!*

Whereas Michael used to run the investigations set-up, a newcomer in the shape of assistant editor Nicholas Lloyd was appointed to the role.

Our relationship was rather strange. Our first chat went like this:

"Ah, a grammar school boy, right?"

"Yes. Nick. And you're from a public school, Oxford and all that, I take it."

As I recall that was it. However, some time later he asked me if I would like to have lunch with the newly appointed education secretary, Margaret Thatcher.

"You could go to Rules," he said, naming the up-market canteen for the elite of the Civil Service.

"Not my kind of diner, Nick. Can't see what I could write about having lunch in a posh restaurant with the schools' boss."

"You know," he said. "Margaret Thatcher – milk snatcher?"

"I'm told she likes the nickname," I told him. "Makes the Tories think she's tough on saving the taxpayers' money."

I don't know how he took that. But for better or worse it proved accurate.

When Nick later became editor of the *Daily Express* he threw the weight of the paper behind her at the polls and she eventually rewarded him with a knighthood.

At this point Tiny Lear was still editor of the *NoW* and neither he nor Nick Lloyd interfered with the John Field column which regularly appeared just as I wrote it – a pretty rare thing in Fleet Street.

Part of the reason for this was the column's huge readership. Our readers were used to chatting to us by letter: our 'Readers Write' page, our competitions, and, of course, the famous Hilton Bureau, all attracted an enormous amount of mail. So I followed tradition, kept the matey tone of the column, and mainly went to bat for the underdog. Back when he was editor, Stafford had given me an assistant to help with replies to readers – Jenny – a pretty good choice as, over a drink, I'd discovered she was from the same Wiltshire village as my father: Steeple Ashton, a relic of England's past, apparently preserved in amber for all time. Jenny had asked me one day if my father had ever claimed relationship to the Lord of the Manor, and when I'd said no, she'd said that he must be the only villager who hadn't. She cleverly designed a code for the letters in our huge mailbag – a big 'R' for regular writer and various other designations, each with a pro-forma reply. In those days if you wanted to get in touch with a reader, the drill was to send a telegram to their home asking them to phone in and to transfer the charge.

There was never any likelihood of my running out of material for the John Field treatment.

Quiet week? Let's see if we can pick something up – so I would ring my favourite MPs or showbiz people (who were always looking for a plug) – and this was long before the cult of celebs really took over the business.

So I phoned Diana Dors: "It's John Field of the *News of the Screws*. What have you got for me this week, darling?"

"Hey, I've got something that's right up your street ..." (a burst of the giggles). She kept interrupting herself, cackling away like some naughty schoolgirl.

It turned out she'd been to visit Alan Lake, her husband, who was serving a year in the pokey for his part in a pub brawl. She'd taken some magazines for him, including a comic – apparently he was a great fan of *The Dandy.*

"Thing is, John ..." (another fit of the giggles) " ... the screw on the gate allowed the magazines ... but carefully locked the comic away in a drawer ..." (more giggles). "Get a copy of this week's Dandy, darling. Right up your alley!"

I did. There on the front page was Korky the Cat, in a suit of broad arrows, banged up for stealing fish. In the last frame he's in the prison yard leaping onto a mattress and bouncing over the walls to freedom, just like George Blake.

I led the column with it – and as a punchline:

'Just as well Alan wasn't allowed to see that ... might have given him ideas, eh?'

Any friend of Korky the Cat is a friend of mine

9

'S'all taken care of, ol' boy'

My time in Fleet Street coincided with the growing acceptance of women reporters, sub-editors, and eventually (shock-horror for a lot of males) editors. Back in the late 1960s you could count on one hand the number of famous national women writers.

The one the *News of the World* took to its heart was undoubtedly Nancy Spain. From a top-class family in Newcastle, she was educated at Roedean and served in the Wrens in World War II. Nancy became a well-known (rather mannish) voice on the BBC, an accomplished sports commentator, and also a popular columnist for the *News of the World* where she dazzled Stafford and everyone else on the paper. She made tragic headlines in 1964 when she was on board an aeroplane, on her way to commentate on the Grand National. The plane inexplicably crashed over Aintree, killing everyone on board.

Around that time, newspapers were beginning to notice the popularity of women columnists on the smarter magazines. On the *NoW* we already had the freelance Rosalie Shann, and among the ranks of young reporters with a foot on the ladder were enterprising girls, plenty keen and capable – like the ones Gabbert and I recruited.

Then suddenly it was was the era of women's-column power: the *Daily Mirror* had the indomitable Marjorie 'Dear Marje' Proops, an agony aunt with a taste for campaigning – for instance on better treatment for rape victims – and always with dedication and compassion for the millions of readers who wrote to her during a lengthy career.

Jean Rook, notably of the *Daily Express,* interviewed a long list of famous figures including Margaret Thatcher, Indira Ghandi and Elizabeth Taylor, and kept her down-to-earth attitude with all of them. She's on record as saying "You know why I'm popular with readers? Because I'm as down to earth as they are."

I once had the pleasure of meeting both Jean Rook and Marje Proops in a pub with my wife Robina. I remember saying to her, "Let's go over to Dirty Dick's", the oyster bar in Liverpool Street. When we got settled with a couple of glasses of bubbly, I realised that at the counter near us were two rather amazing people to bump into: Marje and Jean enjoying a chat together.

I gave the waiter my John Field card and asked him to ask if my wife, the Women's Lib campaigner, could come over to say hello.

"Bring her over," said Marje.

I should have known that John Field would not get another word in ...

More and more women were making their mark in the Street. The *Daily Mail* gave the best part of a page to Lynda Lee-Potter for her column. She'd started life as an actress and liked to share some of her theatrical reminiscences with me whenever we travelled on the same train – me to Southampton and she to Bournemouth – and we Fleet Street males were in some awe of her when she carried on commuting throughout most of a pregnancy.

And then there was Helen Minsky, rocking the celebrities' boat from her safe haven at the Nigel Dempster gossip column on the *Daily Mail* for what seems to have been forever. I'd known her from her youth as a member of our infamous Pompey Mafia – we've shared a number of hair-raising adventures, notably in ski resorts. Minsky (we never called her anything else) became a Saturday casual at the *NoW*, best remembered there for being the first to alert the news desk to the sinking of the Cambridge Eight in the 1978 varsity boat race.

A decade or two later when my son Michael was hired by the

Daily Mail he spotted Minsky at the water cooler and endeared himself to her: "For a moment there I thought you were Helen Minsky – but you are obviously too young."

Towards the end of my sub-editing days at the *NoW* I was often asked to lend a hand to our new women's editor Unity Hall, an old pal of mine: a hard-boiled journalist, she reserved her feminine side for Fleet Street parties. She had been hired to set up a team of women correspondents and it proved a clever move, attracting a big circulation boost.

Even the hardest old-timers in the Street began to show respect for the other sex – and in the years after I left, the *NoW* was to be run by a series of powerful women editors, the last of the line, of course, being Rebekah Brooks.

A columnist thrives on inside information: that was no problem for John Field. I managed with ease to set up an 'information service' from government and parliamentary circles because, as a commuter on the line from Waterloo to Southampton, I regularly travelled in politically august company. The line was also used by the likes of Rear-Admiral Morgan Giles, the long-serving MP for Winchester; Oliver Crosthwaite-Eyre, MP for the New Forest; and Dr Horace King, MP for Southampton Itchen – later Speaker of the House of Commons and who eventually went to the upper chamber as Lord Maybray King.

They were among regular commuters to and from the House, usually travelling in the dining car – and fully paid-up members of the Friday Club, which monopolised the rear end of the bar. The Friday Club had been established by Brian Freemantle, foreign editor of the *Daily Mail,* yours truly, Alistair Stewart the TV newsreader and Jack Frost, an old-timer from the *Daily Telegraph*, who frequently joined us.

So while my Sunday-paper rivals had to spend half their lives hanging around the Commons looking for newsy scraps, I simply travelled in style and kept my ears open. The members all brought special backgrounds to the party, Crosthwaite-Eyre with anecdotes about his time working for Winston Churchill, Rear-Admiral Morgan with his wide network of influential establishment figures, and the rest of us with our Fleet Street anecdotes (some of them even true).

One of Jack Frost's better stories began with a row between a hack and his boss at the *Daily Express* in the ultra-modern building of shiny black glass nicknamed the *Black Lubyanka* after the headquarters of the KGB in Moscow.

Reception hall of the 'Black Lubyanka'

In a fit of bravado the hack wrote his resignation letter and swaggered off to 'Auntie's' pub for a long, liquid lunch. When he finally fell asleep the pub staff tucked him up in a blanket and left him to it. He reckoned he woke up about seven that evening to the clatter of people moving upstairs to the lounge. Feeling rather dry, he followed the crowd to the party and accepted a drink from a waitress.

A tall, rather distinguished chap wished him 'Good Evening' and befuddled as he was, the hack responded with "I know we've met, but can't quite place you ..."

The tall chap smiled:

"Ah, I'm usually known as the Duke of Edinburgh," he said, adding helpfully, "you know, the Queen's husband? Look here's a picture of her."

"And," Frost told us, "he took a 50p piece from his pocket, handed it to our hero and said, 'Here you can keep this – as a reminder.'"

Our usual popular drink on the train was a large G&T, except when we were held up by a flurry of snow, or any one of a hundred excuses such as 'leaves on the line' or 'the wrong kind of snow' dreamed up by British Rail, which meant we generally ordered another round of drinks. Some of those excuses were so unbelievable that Doc King reckoned they were being invented by Freemantle and me on the grounds that we were used to making it all up.

Meeting Doc King, as everyone in Southampton referred to him, was one of the best pieces of luck that came my way: he became a good friend, fed me stories and I helped him out at election time. Early on he learned that – way back in my youth – I had supported the Liberal Party and had also been a friend of Dr Reginald Bennett, the Tory MP for Gosport and Fareham, largely because in his medical life he was a colleague and friend of my girlfriend's mother.

Similarly, on the way to London on the 9.10, I had a number of informed business types to share information with. I used to bring the morning papers with me into the diner and over coffee we'd share them out.

One of my classic train scoops came from a charming Scot, a former Glasgow shipwright, who had a lucrative business in buying ships for scrap.

If Dennis leaned over and said: 'Do you want to buy a battleship?' chances are he wasn't joking. There came a time when he confided in me that he was acting for the government to sell a redundant British warship to the Indian navy. Two days later he took me aside to say the government had cancelled the sale. I start to sympathise, but he whispered:

"No, John. It's not that. It probably means there's going to be another war between India and Pakistan."

And so it happened – what came to be known as the

Bangladesh War (1971). I handed the scoop to Noyes Thomas for Sunday for the *NoW* but I also tipped off Jack Frost for the *Sunday Telegraph* and let them share the story, building up goodwill for a rainy day when I could get a favour out of them – after all, they were hardly our competitors.

Jack was a good friend – he was chairman of the old Press Club in Fleet Street, and the Duke of Edinburgh's press officer for Cowes Week. His pals called him Whispering Jack Frost, on account of a throat problem that had left him husky. Of course, it added to his charm. He lived in a rather nice Art Deco flat round the corner from me in Southampton with his daughter Daphne who was always concerned about him.

From time to time I'd get a phone call from her:

"Hello, John. Dad's going up to town in the morning on the 9.10 – would you keep an eye on him please? He's getting the 6.30 back."

Jack never really needed any help from me. Quite the other way round.

I got to Waterloo one evening to find the 6.30 had been cancelled. I went to phone home and bumped into Jack.

"Don't worry about that," he whispered. "There's a QE2 boat-train leaving at seven. We'll get that."

"But Jack, they won't let us on ..."

"S'all taken care of, ol boy."

I noticed a slight slur and realised he'd had a few. Nevertheless I followed him through the gate and boarded the QE2 boat-train. A steward standing by one of the First Class carriages saluted Jack, took his briefcase and led us into a compartment.

The train duly pulled out at 7pm. And at 7.05 our steward reappeared, towel over his arm, leaned into the compartment and raised an eyebrow ...

"Two large Johnny Walker's – no ice," croaked Jack, and the steward vanished – and as he did so, a chap in a suit knocked on the door.

"Thought I heard you, Jack – can I join you?"

He turned out to be a Bournemouth nightclub owner; pleasant but a bit full of himself. We chatted for a while, interrupted only by the steward with refills all round. Then our friend produced a facsimile newspaper, a popular stunt run by the *Daily Express* – a reproduction of one of theirs from October 1930.

"Those were the days," he said. "You don't get quality writing like this. It's all about the R101 airship disaster ... she suddenly burst into flame, you know, just like that!" snapping his fingers.

"Take a look at page three," Jack whispered. "Have a look at the by-line."

(Rustle of pages turning).

Then he read: "Exclusive by ... Jack Frost." His eyebrows shot up. "Can't possibly be you, can it?"

"How else could I know it was there?" Jack said, and his throaty cackle was something to treasure.

One particular John Field political sally brought me into conflict with Conservative Party headquarters.

The Tories put out the results of an opinion poll among voters which purported to show that an overwhelming proportion would prefer to privatise the National Health Service.

A quick look at my weekly postbag would have given them a much better idea of how ordinary people felt about the NHS. So John Field ran a piece accusing the Tories of asking loaded questions to get the answer they wanted – like the judge asking the man in the dock: "When did you stop beating your wife?"

My piece drew an indignant and rather threatening letter from the pollsters. And I also had a phone call from political writer Frank Johnson, then working for the *Sun*, who had written a follow-up piece agreeing with my attack, and who had also been threatened by the party. We put our heads together and I called a contact at Tory HQ, which promptly produced an invitation for Frank and me to drop in for lunch at their offices off Downing Street.

The lunch was well up to scratch – the wine particularly impressive. And then Frank and I outlined our strategy: we would either run a similar poll (but with no loaded questions) to test public opinion for ourselves, or we'd both look for an opportunity to publicise some aspect of Tory policy in the near future.

Naturally the politicos agreed to part two – and we shook hands all round. It's the way it works.

I operated the John Field column in two ways – by ridiculing government and local councils for their mistakes that cost the taxpayers millions, and by picking up the odd behaviour of everybody else, the funnier the better.

When the former Royal Navy supremo Lord Louis Mountbatten protested at the continual mothballing of our once powerful fleets, I backed the old salt to the hilt. And I finished with this comment on a current story ....

A British ship with the proud name of Admiral Nelson carrying, wait for it, a cargo of fertiliser, managed to hurl herself aground off the Norfolk coast – out of shame?

Another topic I tackled was when Southampton citizens had bravely taken the town council to the High Court because they didn't want to lose a part of their historic, beautiful common to a nasty tarmac car park. Against all the usual odds of ordinary folk taking on The Establishment, and against all precedents, the proletariat had won the day. The council then spitefully hit back, saying they would have to stop all traditional fairs and shows on the common. A huge outcry of *'Sour Grapes'* from John Field and the council caved in.

Then there was the man in Kent who had had central heating installed at considerable cost. A plumber had three goes at fixing a fault in the water supply. But it still made a noise 'like the hammers of hell.' The heating company chief advised: 'If it doesn't stop shove a matchstick in the ballcock valve."

'Great, isn't it?' said John Field. 'Several hundred quid and it runs on a dead match'.

And this:

An American soldier in Vietnam was awarded the Purple Heart – the medal Uncle Sam gives to all GIs wounded in battle. Unfortunately it turned out this squaddie got his wound in a brothel – bitten by a girl enemy agent.

'Enough to make a British Royal Marine faint clean away,' said John Field.

One night I dropped in to the Three Tuns, a pub I used at Romsey, a few miles from home. Jeannie the landlady poured my pint and casually mentioned I'd just missed Prince Phillip.

She was quite used to the occasional royal dropping in, the pub being just across the road from Broadlands, stately home of Lord Louis Mountbatten.

The difference here was that Prince Philip was alone in the bar. He had a glass of sherry, made it last, and ordered another, but still no-one else came in. "Where is everyone?" he asked. Jeannie pointed out that it was only 6.30pm and most people didn't come in much before seven.

The story appeared in John Field's column, of course, under the headline 'Lonely Sailor?' A familiar call to matelots from girls in Pompey.

Last time I went into the Tuns the cutting, yellow with age, was still pinned up over the bar.

10

Divorce By Post!

B ack when I was still on the *Southern Daily Echo* and wanted to buy my own house, I had sought the advice of Rodney Andrew, my editor, about getting a solicitor. He'd recommended a chap I shall call Greg Smart.

I had taken his advice and Greg and I had become friends. Over the years he'd acted for me in a number of property deals and had also become a valuable source of information.

He also had some interesting quirks.

One night we walked into a busy bar at a New Forest hotel. He stopped dead in his tracks, wheeled me around and headed back the way we'd come in.

"Wass up, Greg? "

He said nothing until we were well outside the place, then lightened up.

"That loud-voiced woman in the fur coat," he said. "Chairman of one of the New Forest courts ... best avoided."

And that was the sort of thing that happened, often enough to indicate he had a real phobia about people he might meet in the course of his business. At this point I should reveal that most of his work involved standing up in court, defending men (and sometimes women) accused of criminal offences. He had a pretty good record of getting them off, too.

Of course, if the magistrates directed that the case be tried higher up the system, Greg was obliged to work with a barrister since solicitors could not be heard in the higher courts.

Every now and again he would come up with a story interesting to the *NoW* and he would pass the details on to me.

And actually he had the reporter's eye for the bizarre. There was the professional burglar who left his half-eaten sandwich on the safe he'd just emptied, complete with a perfect impression of his crooked front teeth – the clue that gave the police an easy collar and him a stiff sentence.

Or the story of the man who walked into a pub with a six-inch nail protruding from the top of his head. That one went round the world – and as far as I know no-one ever found out how the victim survived, or whodunnit.

The best scoop ever for our partnership was the further relaxation in the early 70s of the rules governing divorce between consenting parties. Greg spotted a clause in the many volumes of legislation, some in force, some awaiting ratification, and called me in a state of high excitement. When he calmed down he explained that one interesting part of the new divorce rules had been triggered by the passing into law of another part.

It was complex but Greg explained that this sort of legislation was rather like the setting of an alarm on a clock ... click to the trigger point and off goes the alarm.

And the upshot, as Greg spotted – and many another lawyer apparently did not – that it meant, as the *News of the World* succinctly summed it up in the following Sunday's splash:

DIVORCE BY POST!

The leader of the divorce bar even sent Greg a telegram, congratulating him on spotting the significance.

Tiny Lear and Nick Lloyd between them did me the favour of a lifetime. Tiny wanted to run a series by George Wigg, a former minister in Harold Wilson's government.

Wigg, a long-serving army officer until he became an MP, was appointed Paymaster General by Wilson, but this was merely a cover for special duties such as liaising with MI5 and anything considered 'hush hush'.

In 1967 he had been appointed chairman of the Horserace Betting Levy Board and left Parliament as life peer Baron Wigg.

Nick Lloyd told me Wigg would bring in his notes for a series on his work as Harold Wilson's aide and on general items of interest from his colourful past. I would work from these notes and meet him regularly for a chat to get the right flow for the series, which was to run over a number of weeks.

Lord Wigg told a good tale and his story was obviously of interest to our readers. The mailbag surged, right from the first week.

However it was also one of the most important friendships of my life. I found Lord Wigg a fascinating companion; we took to taking a quiet corner in a Fleet Street wine bar in mid-afternoon when we had the place more or less to ourselves. He was obviously aware of my friendship with Southampton MP Doc King.

"I'd say you're a young man prepared to take a gamble," he told me.

Bearing in mind that he loved horse racing, clearly he knew what he was talking about.

"I think I can help you to earn a great deal of money if you are prepared to take a chance," he said, capturing my interest and then some.

"If I were you, I'd borrow every penny I could. Make some rock-solid investments and you could double, or even treble your money in five years starting from now," he told me.

I told him I owned my own house, a comfortable Edwardian villa, on a council mortgage. I had a good salary from the *NoW*, topped up by some freelance work for *Flame*, the sophisticated and lavishly designed staff magazine of Southern Gas, a contract I'd acquired in 1962 from one of the *Southern Evening Echo*'s leading writers, Tom Hickman, when he left the area to become editor of *TV Times*. Besides that, my wife Robina had a respectable salary from teaching.

"Do you run a car?" he asked.

"Yeah, I've got an old and much-loved Humber with a bench

front seat and a column gear-change."

"Well my advice is to buy a brand new car on the never-never. Don't bother to sell the Humber – you can afford to hang on to it for as long as you like, but don't spend any money on it."

Another time he asked: "Are there any modern, new-builds in the offing in Southampton?"

"There's some Wimpey-style modern town houses due to go up in Bassett, the posh part of the city," I said.

On George's advice I went to take a look, and the houses I was interested in turned out to be in the same road where my Fleet Street travelling companion Brian Freemantle of the *Daily Express* lived. I regarded this as a good omen.

These were three-bedroom town houses, with a lawned frontage, a drive and a garage. A reasonable-sized rear garden backed onto woodland to the north of Southampton – as far as I was aware, the next big city going north was Birmingham. The brochures looked pretty good – and there were opportunities to have some alterations to the plan. The location also looked interesting since Yolanda, Rosemary and Michael were all at the same school a short cycle-ride away across the sports centre.

"Ideal," Robina said when I showed her the plan.

And she set to work dreaming up alterations to the layout – for instance having the children's bunk beds built-in – among a host of changes to the kitchen, bathroom, shower-room and toilets.

Among my assets George found a life/pension plan with Sun Life of Canada that had been sold to me (and several other young reporters) by an ex-cub reporter who'd quit journalism for the better salary. Thanks, mate. I'd had the policy since 1955 and its dividends had been covering the annual fees for the last ten years. So in effect it was costing me nothing and growing nicely.

George suggested turning this into an insurance mortgage to buy the house (the market price being £7,500). The upshot of this was that I got the house for about £150 down, plus the annual insurance premium – which was so little I can't remember it – and still managed to keep the first house.

So far, so good.

"This is a great idea, George," I told him.

"Ah," he told me with a wink, "I haven't told you the best bit. You may have noticed that the money men, British, European and American, are all forecasting a big rise in inflation over the next few years?"

" I could hardly miss it – it's been in all the papers and TV."

"Well," he said, "I've learned that this inflation will be bigger than anything we've seen since the fall of the German Mark in the 1920s."

He was right. And I can tell you that I sold my new house four years later for £12,500, paying back the original £7,500 and pocketing £5,000. Not a housing-market bubble: just simple, roaring inflation.

In the intervening four years I had let the old house to four young men, three of whom paid rent to the managing tenant who lived rent-free. My two successive managers had had the sense to put the equivalent of the rent into the bank each month. Peter bought a very nice flat and the one who took over from him, nicknamed 'Hairy Dick,' later moved to Canada and bought himself a little house on a ranch.

Robina and I moved back into our spacious Edwardian villa, treated it to a complete refurb and – appropriately – filled the garden with roses.

Oh, yes and I bought the new car; a Citroen Dyane priced at £750 and we went for a family jaunt round Ireland in it. I bought it, as George had recommended, on the never-never, paying so much a month.

Nine years later I was driving down a country road when a limb of a beech tree broke away and fell on the car. I braked and simultaneously managed to duck under the dashboard. My Dyane was clearly a write-off.

I went to the nearest house and a charming lady made some tea and handed me the phone so I could report the crash to the police.

Amazingly quickly, a traffic cop was knocking at the door: "Where's the driver?" he asked. I told him it was me and he said "Good God I'd thought you'd be dead. Come and see your smashed-up car."

He took me out to the wreck – there was blood all over the front seat but miraculously all I had was a cut finger that didn't even need sewing up.

The insurance company paid the full price of £750 and I also negotiated with Hampshire County Council on the grounds that their roadside tree had crushed my lovely Dyane and received full compensation – of £750.

To my astonishment when I tried to give the insurers their £750 back, they told me to keep it. My clever bank manager in Ludgate Hill (just off Fleet Street) worked out that over nine years that car had cost me only £2 a week.

And this was all down to Lord Wigg, God bless him.

Oh, I forgot to say, I also borrowed £200 from Mr Murdoch – to be repaid after two years. Of course, after two years, Rupert generously lent me another £200.

Fleet Street bank managers were case-hardened to the problems and trials journalists put themselves through. We weren't the easiest customers.

The first one at Lloyd's in Ludgate Hill (I'll call him Mr Stephenson) took me on in 1960 when I joined the American news agency, Associated Press. Later he saw me through the trauma of emigrating to France to join the AFP news agency in Paris – and my hasty return a few months later escaping the fighting in the streets.

When he retired he asked me to find him a nice little cottage on the Hampshire coast. I got pretty close: I found him a lovely old place in Dorset. I used to get cards from him, thanking me for finding his dream cottage.

Bank manager number two was Young Mr Quelch (another pseudonym, of course) who used to like to lunch in the Press Club, and I found no problem in taking him there; he was a truly charming man. But he was the man in charge when I had to repay some advance expenses I'd drawn from the *NoW* to go on a job – and somehow one of his clerks refused to honour the cheque. Naturally this did not look good back at Bouverie Street.

What to do about it?

I hit upon a good wheeze. I got Ted, one of our freelance photographers, to come with me to Ludgate Hill, and I armed myself with a horsewhip (borrowed from the display in a leather shop in Old Holborn).

I went noisily into the bank, brandishing my whip and demanding the manager come and get his punishment. I'd picked a good moment when there were only a couple of customers – and the staff went into a sort of frozen state.

Quelch came out, saw that it was me, and called me into his office.

"No," I declared, "I want you out on Ludgate Hill so that people see you get the horse-whipping you deserve for ruining my reputation."

His secretary intervened: "Shall I call the police, Mr Q?"

"Good God, no. I shall take my medicine like a man," he said.

And out onto Ludgate Hill we went, where he and I posed for Ted's picture, the end of the whip curling round Quelch's shoulders and me snarling like a sadistic brute.

Ted headed downhill to sell the pic to the *Evening Standard*. Quelch wrote a cheque to the *NoW* and we both went off to a decent lunch at the Press Club.

My third manager, Mr Simpson as I will call him here, used to sing in the choir at St Bride's. In many ways he had the toughest job because, having started in the days of the 'special relationship' enjoyed between bank and customer, he found himself presiding over the profound change to the heartless, faceless system of the late twentieth century – a change with which he was distinctly out of tune.

When the end of Fleet Street was looming up over Wapping, Mr Simpson wrote inviting me to a party at the bank, marking a landmark for Lloyds. The guests were largely representatives of big companies. Hitherto, Ludgate branch had been a bank for smaller private accounts, but these had almost all gone.

Simpson greeted me and led me across the room to a chap about my age.

"Mr John Bull meet Mr John Bull," he said – twice. We had both been with Ludgate Hill branch for more than 20 years – and neither of us had been aware of the other. My namesake was in business on his own account and we were the very last private customers of the branch. The end of an era.

11

The Inkies and Me

Here I have a confession to make – I had made a personal pact of friendship with the inkies. There, I've said it. In Fleet Street, journalists generally thought of themselves as the elite and looked down on the humble inkies. It was a nasty social disease I never caught.

It happened like this. I had served my reporter's apprenticeship alongside the print apprentices at Portsmouth. The young journos and the inkies drank in the same pubs, knew the same girls. It was the same when I was on the *Bath Chronicle*, where in the relaxed air of the West Country, we worked together and played together.

Hanging out with the inkies

Soon after I joined the *NoW*, Stafford asked me if I knew my way around the stone (a metal table that holds the frame of the page in type – originally a piece of flat stone as in Caxton's day – which to the printers in my era wasn't all that far back).

I strolled out into the (to me heavenly) ink-incensed air of the big composing room with its batteries of clacking Linotype machines, each with a keyboard to turn raw copy into metal slugs of type – and each fitted with a pot of molten metal to do the job.

As the pages were made up ready to go to press, the stone sub-editor would hang around reading the type (back to front and upside down in the page, of course) before a papier-mâché impression was made, which was then used to make a copy in hot metal. This was later fitted to the huge rotary press, fed by endless rolls of paper, that printed the finished product.

The compositors stood ranged along one side of the great steel make-up slabs. As I went along the line looking for the news pages, one of the comps pointed to me and hollered: "Look out – it's Mac the Knife."

It was an old mate from the *Bath Chronicle*, widely known as 'the only weekly paper that comes out every day'. When my first daughter, Yolanda, was born she had been one of three *Chronicle* babes that arrived that week and, of course, we otherwise useless husbands had all repaired to the pub after maternity visiting hours. I'd earned the nickname 'Mac the Knife' back then because of my full 'naval' beard which the comps said made me look sinister.

I'd continued to bond with the 'comps' even though I'd moved to Fleet Street: in fact I even managed to sell one of them a sailing dinghy I'd outgrown. I was often invited to join them for some special celebration, in their exclusive rendezvous in the basement of the Reuters building, where I was expected to pay for a crate of bottled ale – their tipple of choice for workers in a hot, dry (and, as some would say, truly Satanic) mill.

Many times on a Saturday, when a must-have headline wouldn't fit, I'd be asked by whoever was on the back bench to step out to the composing room and 'have a chat.' These guys had wonderful ways of making solid metal type 'elastic' – if you were a pal, that is.

One of my long-lasting little Saturday chores was the weather forecast. Most papers still seem to neglect this important item as a ploy to gain reader loyalty. But I was convinced, and still am, that newspaper buyers are subliminally influenced by a weather forecast that is 'Sunny', rather than one that offers a miserable, dripping wet day, or – even worse – 'wet and windy'. And this was especially true on Sundays, a day off and a potential day out for most people.

Bull's Theorem preached that the weather panel should always be above the front page fold on the newspaper stand – to sell the paper by subliminal auto-suggestion. It should therefore always start with 'SUNNY' even if the truth had to follow: 'after early showers' or 'sunny spells, rain later'.

That was my *News of the World* forecast, every Saturday for nearly 20 years.

And when the paper finally moved to Wapping with its new technology that made metal-type printing redundant, my pals the printers ceremoniously presented me with the now redundant headline block.

I still have it on display at home among my little treasures.

And then there was The *News of the World* Joke (there was just the one) concerning Jonah, the night stone sub. One midsummer sweltering Saturday night when all composing-room printers were sweating and longing for the shift to end, one of them nipped down the back stairs to the pub across the way to give Jonah the nod to come up and send the paper to bed.

Jonah, perspiring like anyone else, quickly ticked off the sport pages and then leaned over the front page to check the dateline, his last chore. As he did so, his open shirt fell away from his sweaty body and he came into contact with the inked metal. The headline

MILLION POUND
DIAMOND RAID
AT AIRPORT

... came out the right way round on Jonah ...
... the wrong way round on Jonah's wife ...
... the right way round on the milkman ...
... and the wrong way round on the milkman's horse.

History has it that the *Sun* was a runaway success from Day One. But that really wasn't the case. The early days were dogged by a certain lack of cohesion – apart, that is, from the editorial set-up which to all intent and purposes went straight into overdrive.

Yes, the Page 3 Stunners had a lot to do with this, but by far the biggest change was in the editorial staff.

Chief was (Albert) Larry Lamb and his faithful assistant Bernard Shrimsley and they were looking for up-and-coming new boys and girls who could by relied upon to break new ground in newspaper stories.

For instance they appointed Brian McConnell as the first news editor. Brian was an old pal from my days on the *South London Press*, when he was a hard-working freelance covering the south of the city – I remember that he and his wife both drove matching colourful sports cars. A better idea of his qualities will be understood when I remind you that he was the chap who leapt in the way of a bullet when a deranged gunman tried to kidnap Princess Anne in Pall Mall in 1974. McConnell was shot in the chest but made a good recovery and was awarded the Queen's Gallantry Medal.

In Brian's first days as editor, I bumped into him on the landing outside the *Sun* newsroom, with Glen Goody, a reporter who – when he was a junior – I'd taken in as a lodger when I was with the Southampton *Echo*. After introductions all round, Brian sent him into the newsroom, then turned to me.

"He's looking for a job. Is he any good?"

"Not a great innovator as yet – but knows his stuff and is totally reliable," I said. And Goody got the job.

Years later I reminded Glen about that day, but he wouldn't accept that I had anything to do with his appointment. That's human nature, I guess.

Rupert wanted a younger, keener crew and his top men Lamb and Bernard Shrimsley followed through. Instead of the usual Fleet Street custom of poaching people with talent from other papers, they went for younger reptiles looking for a way to the top. The new recruits were a different breed. Back then, we all wore suits to work, but it wasn't long before T-shirts and jeans were the standard uniform, especially for the night crew. They wore anoraks and trainers to and from the office, not overcoats and polished shoes. The reporters and anyone likely to be out-and-about meeting the public stayed with the suits, of course, but us backroom boys were soon decked out in bell-bottomed trousers, wide belts and afghan waistcoats. The new recruits were well paid – but I couldn't imagine any of them wanting to buy an old rectory in Kent. More like they'd be buying vintage cars and doing them up.

At the *News of the World* we kept a pretty close eye on changes at the *Sun* as a clue to the way Rupert wanted to go. It wasn't long, for example, before our Saturday casuals, subs or reporters, were mostly recruited from *Sun* staff.

Once upon a time, as all good legends begin, we welcomed a newcomer called Kelvin MacKenzie to do a Saturday shift. It was the start of a beautiful, though sometimes stormy, partnership as Kelvin rose to being boss of Britain's most popular paper and popular fame.

Years later, as the brilliant – though often controversial – editor of the *Sun*, he recruited my son Michael to his first Fleet Street job. And he told him this story about me:

"It was my first Saturday shift," he said, "and your dad was on the back bench. The chief sub suggested your dad take me for a break – and off we went to the Peanut Parlour. After a couple of pints and a series of tales about the old days on the *Screws*, he wound up with 'You'd better get back early as it's your first day'.

"Back in the office I slumped back into my chair saying 'God, what a bore – is he always like that?'

"Hoots of glee all round the table. I was baffled until chief sub Monty Levy said: 'You mean he didn't tell you his family motto – Bore Him Before He Bores You?'"

Thank you, Kelvin.

As the *Sun* boys got their feet under the table and saw they were starting to pull in the public, a revolution in newspapers was underway. A lot of aristocratic heads rolled over the next few years as the other tabloids joined in the dance – and the *Mirror* were busting a gut to keep up. Meanwhile we still had the *NoW* to get out – and at first there was a feeling in the air that we had to sell more to make up for the initial slowness of *Sun* sales, the 'Soaraway *Sun*' being some way down the pike. When Rupert took over the *NoW* we had raised the circulation by half-a-million within the first six months or so: the *Sun* took a bit longer – but it happened.

I was comfortably ensconced in our features office with a remit to edit copy provided by Trevor Kempson and the freelances on our books including Simon Regan. Also on the team were the hard-grafting Ray Chapman who, before getting into the newspaper game, had worked on liners operating from Southampton including the Cunard QE2 – as a hairdresser. Of course we all took advantage of his talent to get our haircuts regularly in the office.

One of our early triumphs was the story of a steward who attracted the attention of the proverbial rich widow who tended to use the ocean liners as an hotel. Living in Southampton, I had heard rumours of this grand lady who poured money all over her favourite steward, and eventually led him down the aisle. I spent a fair bit of my time in waterfront bars, trying to get a line on this bloke. Everyone had heard the rumour, but no-one had anything concrete to go on, until one day a well-dressed chap walked into our front office in Bouverie Street and asked to speak to Trevor Kempson. You guessed it – it was the steward wanting to sell his story.

Trevor and Ray took him through the highlights of his time at sea in all its wonderful romantic fascination. Eventually they handled the raw copy over to me to edit.

There was so much detail and some wonderful coincidences – it truly was a story tailor-made for *News of the World* readers. I sweated blood trying to find the right tone of voice for the steward and how to make a splash with the intro – enough to do the thing justice.

In the end I had him standing in line with his wonderful wife waiting to be introduced to the master of the QE2:

"Have we met before? Your face is very familiar."

"Yes, sir, I used to make your favourite cocktail for you when I was chief steward. May I introduce my wife?" ... then the story swiftly went into how his luck had changed. It ran for a couple of weeks and brought in an amazing amount of mail.

Occasionally Tiny Lear would come up with an idea for me to follow up.

"You interested in Shakespeare, John?"

"Only the comedies, Tiny," I confessed.

"Well the American actor Sam Wanamaker wants to build a replica of The Globe on the site of Shakespeare's original theatre."

I met Mr Wanamaker in a pub on the South Bank – which was so old it could have been used as a set for an Elizabethan tavern.

We sat over a coal fire discussing his dream and the feasibility of getting round the stringent planning laws of twentieth-century cities, the red tape, the colossal extent of lawyers' fees and all the many, many obstacles in his way.

"It's going to be a long-term project then," I said.

"I'm sure it will be. I don't expect it to happen quickly," he said.

In fact it took nearly 30 years before the new Globe was officially opened by the Queen and by then Sam had been dead four years.

12

A Bit of a Shoe Fetish

The *News of* had been changing since Stafford's day. Old hands left, new ones arrived. The layout system began to change, slowly at first, but inevitably the *Sun* had its effect. The arguments raged between those who were in favour of a change from broadsheet to tabloid format and those who wanted to 'stick to a winning formula.' Personally, I didn't think there was a future for the *NoW* if it became just another tabloid with celebrities and girls exposing their tits.

The subs room was now led by former *Daily Sketch* chief sub John Smyth, a very bright guy with a wicked sense of humour. He had replaced Ron Lawrence, who had moved into the composing room as editorial linkman.

One of our new assets was a layout artist called Bric Wilkins – a designer who added more than a touch of artistry to the paper – who had studied art at a London college and also taught graphic art in a school. We became friends, both having wives in what Robina called 'the art lark'.

About this time the course leader at the Regent Street Poly was looking for help, so I took the chance to earn a bit extra by lecturing on one of my spare mornings. It wasn't long before I recruited Bric to the place as well. And eventually Freddie Hodgson, Bric's layout boss at the *NoW*, a long-serving northerner, was also taken on part time. Freddie was later commissioned to write a textbook under the patronage of the National Council for the Training of Journalists and I believe he did well out of it.

I once asked him to lend me some notes for a lecture I been asked to give in Southampton.

Freddie snorted. "Well this is valuable stuff. How much will you pay me?"

I walked away – I didn't even mention the fact that he owed his foot on that ladder to my help at the Poly. Some of the mean sons of Yorkshire do their countrymen no favours at all.

However, years later, the *Sunday Times* ran a jokey back-page competition for an update of that famous Yorkshire old saw:

"Eyt all, sup all, pay nowt;
And if ivver tha does owt fer nowt
Allus do it for thessen."

I thought this was too good to miss. My entry ran:

"Eyt all, sup all, pay nowt;
And if tha does owt
Do it wi tha mouth."

I won first prize. Thank you *Sunday Times* (a Murdoch publication).

I'd first done some work for the Regent Street Poly after I left the *Mirror.*

A chap called Ray Boston had been running a journalism course, partly financed by the Colonial Office (when we still had a couple of colonies left) and my group of students had been exotic, to say the least. It had included a tall, very dark, beautiful young woman with a decidedly regal manner. At all times she had been accompanied by a hefty male security man, who probably carried a sidearm, but who had sat silent and watchful at the back of any room she was in.

She was, in fact, the princess of a governing tribe in one of our former dominions in Africa. Of course she spoke perfect English, something that under other circumstances I'd have said I found out by chatting to her – but the fact was that you did not chat to the princess: you addressed her as Your Highness and you waited until she began the conversation.

Me: "My compliments, Your Highness – may I ask whether you have any particular preferences in regard to my programme for the coming term which I have circulated to all students?"

Prinny: "My advisers tell me it is all perfectly in order. I shall endeavour to carry out the work you ask of me to the best of my ability. As I have done in my other studies in the UK. Thank you ..."

I had been clearly dismissed. But over lunch in the pub I'd asked Ray Boston what other studies she meant and he'd told me – with great satisfaction – she had a double first in classics and also a law degree. Blimey.

Another exotic had been the amiable young Persian whose father owned Tehran's biggest daily paper: he too had been an excellent student. Some years later, at the time when the revolt against the Shah was building up, I caught a BBC TV programme in which my former student was interviewed, and introduced as the editor of said newspaper. That was the last time I'd heard anything of him – perhaps he was one of the many liquidated in the revolution and the birth of Iran.

The student I had got to know best was David Zinian from Lebanon – a very quick learner, very much in the mould of Ray Boston and me – a naturally enterprising young man with a bright future ahead. For a few years we had exchanged Christmas cards, but I'd followed his career later in life when as a foreign editor I'd read his bulletins on the wire during the long civil wars in Lebanon where he was doing an excellent job for the American news agency BUP. And I'd always used his stories.

When I'd walked into the Poly on the morning of Friday October 21, 1966 I'd found Boston and some of the staff listening to the BBC news of disaster at the Pantglas junior school in the Welsh village of Aberfan. A mudslide from the huge slag-heap behind the village had engulfed the school, suffocating the best part of a generation of children.

My students had just stood in the corridor listening to the radio, white-faced, clearly in shock. Ray Boston and I had had a quick word in his office – and I'd suggested we got them working, maybe attempt to get a news-sheet out, based on BBC reports as they came in, and maybe an update when the early editions of the evening papers hit the streets.

We'd divided the students up into writing, editing, and background groups, plus a production group using our new, sophisticated (for its time) copy printer and the two best typists in the place. Our first edition had been on the streets just after 11am – with a billboard drawn up by the princess:

MUDSLIDE
HITS SCHOOL:
MANY DEAD

Scrappy though our first edition had been, it sold fast – at a shilling a time. By the time we'd got more details from the lunchtime papers, plus our own map of the disaster location, the students had been – emotionally and mentally – sinking or swimming in their first taste of 'real' journalism.

Did it help their careers?

Recently I was chatting to another old Pompey Mafia mate, Trevor Fishlock and his wife Penny, both of *The Times*. Trevor and I were exchanging tales from our early days, and then it was Penny's turn ...

"I was a student on the old Journalism course at the Regent Street Poly," she said.

"Ah, yes, " I said. "I did a stint as a lecturer there with Ray Boston – would have been in the mid-60s, I suppose."

"Yeah," Penny agreed, "I suppose it was. I remember it was about the time of the Aberfan school disaster, you know – the mud slide," said Penny. "We got a news-sheet out and sold it to students and passers-by ..." She tailed off, staring at me. "It was you!" she cried, pointing a finger at me across the dinner table.

"Guilty," I said, gobsmacked.

And as if that wasn't typical of British journalism, I've got more news for you – the first national newspaper reporter on the disaster scene was .... Stafford Somerfield of the *News of the World.*

I was always on the lookout for interesting people to write about; I used to pride myself on being a man of the world (know what I mean?) – until I met Susan.

My Saturday shift usually ended at 11pm, leaving me ample time to get the midnight train home to Southampton. Few people travelled on this one and most of them dropped off to sleep. Often I had a compartment to myself, until one night a smartly dressed young woman peered in, weighed me up and diffidently asked if she could join me.

Susan lived with her husband, a Southampton businessman.

"Oh, and I'm also a working girl," she said pointedly.

She knew I was a journalist and would therefore recognise the slang for a prostitute. Naturally I asked her to tell me about it.

"Swear on your mother's grave you won't write about me."

I did. And over the next few weeks I got the whole tale. She wasn't Miss Whiplash – the famous dominatrice who spawned dozens of copycats – or anything like it, but elements of the story were similar. Susan had a flat not far from lawyer-land. She had a maid (herself an ex-pro, now retired). And a friendly copper or two, not as clients but for security. No money changed hands, Susan assured me; it was simply an age-old, sensible arrangement to give her and the coppers a comfortable life.

I'd worked in London long enough to know these things went on, but Susan still made me blink.

I asked about the clients. Cagey at first, she decided to explain how it worked, basing it on one of her regulars. Regular indeed: he dropped by every Thursday afternoon at six, and was duly admitted by the maid. He and Susan would undress and then he would crawl on all fours to pose in front of her dressing table. Susan, wearing only a negligée, would sit alongside him and brush her hair.

"Thirty-six times to the left, then thirty-six times to the right. Always the same, never more, never less. We'd get dressed, he'd give me a kiss on the cheek, hand me the money, and leave."

She had similar stories of strange performances and I wondered how new clients explained their 'requirements.'

"Oh, some are shy," she said, "but I can usually tell, after chatting a while, what sort of kink a bloke might have, and then we take it from there."

I wasn't totally convinced, until the next time I travelled home with her a few weeks later. She was late getting on the train and I thought she wasn't coming. Then I saw her trying to run down the platform carrying two big bags. I helped her on board.

"What's in the bags?" I said.

"Shoes," she said when she got her breath back. "I've brung some sexy high heels to show you – think you might like it."

With the carriage to ourselves, she haughtily paraded up and down in one glittery, glossy, fascinating pair of heels after another. About a dozen, at least. But who's counting? I don't think I've enjoyed a train ride so much.

"So I have a shoe fetish, darling."

"Don't worry – there's no cure," she said. "Just enjoy."

Over the months we travelled together I found I became more aware of the inner Susan. Of course she was a South London girl with all its tribal taboos and customs deeply in place, much like any other woman from south of the river that I'd known. However, as I knew her better, I sometimes caught a sour note amid the banter. For instance she'd often refer to suicide:

"Well if things get bad there's always Hurry Curry ... or Suety Pud ..."

13

In Some Sunday Papers

As the daily *Sun* was beginning to shake up Fleet Street, I was beginning to try something different. At this time I was comfortably ensconced in the *NoW* features office – but the old Trevor Kempson-style exposé was losing its shock effect on the nation and the customers were looking for new sensations.

Beside this, the top neddies on the *Sun*, Larry Lamb and Bernard Shrimsley, announced that they were 'going to give editor Tiny Lear a hand.' Maybe they should have waited until Tiny asked them.

The change meant that we ran a number of less-than-earth-shaking stories such as the ill-treatment of animals just for the delectation of the rich man's table – all very worthy, but better left to the heavies like the *Guardian* or the *Sunday Times.*

I recall finding a page proof of the feature on my desk. The only thing that Larry Lamb had done was to circle round the French phrase 'blanquette de veau' and to scrawl: "veal is neither white nor creamy". Interfering git – and ignorant with it.

Significantly, from the time of Tiny Lear's retirement in 1974, no fewer than six *NoW* editors went through the revolving door in less than ten years. Stafford had lasted 10 years (1960-1970); Tiny for four. They were to be followed by Peter Stephens and Bernard Shrimsley – both good editors – then the less-than-memorable Kenneth Donlan and Barry Askew; and then in 1981 by Derek Jameson.

Peter Stephens had wanted to hire me as a reporter for his

Newcastle Chronicle back in 1961. Because I was living in Bath he had interviewed me in the offices of the *Chronicle*'s sister paper in Cardiff. We got on very well and I was looking forward to working for him. But before I was due to join, I got a sudden offer of a well-paid job at the American news agency Associated Press in London which, as a responsible husband and father, I could not refuse.

"So I've got you at last," Peter said over a drink in his office. We got along just fine until he moved back to the *Sun* a bit later: in due course he was appointed editorial director of News Group Newspapers.

Over a pint or two I used to compare our two sister papers: to us the daily was Limping Charlie the scruffy-looking greyhound – and the Sunday paper was a pedigree racehorse in Lord Rosebery's colours and matchless over the sticks, as our racing correspondent Stan Agate might have said.

Around this time a very strange opportunity popped up. My sideline for Southern Gas had expanded into writing public relations stories, speeches for the bosses and scriptwriting for their popular 'rah-rah' shows for the workers; I was also thinking of writing a play, a comedy perhaps. A fellow commuter, Bob Scott – a showbiz executive for the great Bernard (later Lord) Delfont – appointed himself as my 'agent' to find me work writing jokes or additional dialogue, usually for big outfits such as Brylcreem or Shell to entertain and inform their workers. Well you have to start somewhere.

When I told David Gordois, the letters page editor and features layout man, about this, he invited me for a drink.

"Look," Gordois said when we met, "keep this to yourself – I'm thinking of trying to get a musical comedy off the ground featuring the *News of the World*. I've come up against the problem of possibly being sued by the company."

Where did I come in? Obviously Gordois saw me as a solver of little problems like that. I was flattered. I nearly told him he was confiding in the wrong bloke – but then I had a great idea. We would do the show, but set it in the 1890s to avoid any contemporary libels.

From then we met regularly in pubs away from the Street. We spent hours going over the plot – Gordois was down to research stories from the Naughty Nineties, such as the shocking divorce of a peer of the realm, while I would pen some lyrics for the real showbiz talent to refine.

I had the bright idea of using that very rude rugby song as an opening number ...

> *In some Sunday papers – we read of the capers*
> *of dustmen and drapers ...*

And then as a swipe to the topical, I dreamed up *The Umbrella Song*, a ditty about the London murder of a foreign spy. The lyric went something like this:

> *He was foully done to death*
> *With his own umbrella ...*
> *And I believe that it was rainin' at the time – boom,*
> *boom!*

On the train one quiet evening I ventured to interest Bob in the idea of the musical and I sang the opening number and chorus, told him a bit about the plot set in the Naughty Nineties ... and about *The Umbrella Song*. He managed to keep a straight face and then insisted that I come and 'do a run-thru' for the great man himself, Bernard Delfont.

I protested that I didn't have enough to go on, but Bob said that would be all the better as 'Father' (as his staff called him) liked to be in on the ground floor of any new enterprise. In fact this proved to be true: the great impresario never batted an eyelid, but smiled and told me to get on with the 'book' of the show.

Every now and again I'd give David a prod and ask him if he had any more ideas. I made a few suggestions, too. Once as we walked down the Strand I pointed up to the facade of a theatre –

"Hey, that could be us up there with our names in lights, David!"

He sounded enthusiastic enough, but the truth is that whatever stopped him, despite all the encouragement from me and from Bob, he never penned a line or came up with any ideas. Or if he did, he never shared them with me.

Bob Scott and one or two people in the know suggested I try it alone or find a new partner, but I how could I just drop Gordois when the whole idea of the show was his baby?

So I soldiered on with some other ideas of my own. I showed a couple of sample scripts to Bob and he urged me to go on writing short plays for radio or TV. And so I took his advice.

Just as well that I was looking to branch out – because when Peter Stephens moved on, the new regime decided to drop the John Field column in favour of a regular piece by a new bloke from the *London Evening News*, a pleasant enough cove, Phil Wrack. His column often featured anecdotes about his holidays in Ireland ... and I can't remember anything else worth comment.

I was moved back to the subs' desk, under the chief sub John Smythe. I really didn't fit in with the editorial policy of the paper under the new editor, Bernard Shrimsley: our features were beginning to concentrate more on showbiz people and pop stars, and the cult of CELEBRITY was beginning to dazzle the media. It was the shape of things to come, of course, but millions of *NoW* readers were not yet ready for that. I had a distinct impression when talking to our new leaders that if they met some of our readers face-to-face they wouldn't know what to say to them.

One of the rules of the old Carr ownership – and one which had remained unchanged – was the provision of a sabbatical for staff writers with five years on the clock. I raised the topic with Peter Stephens before he moved upstairs and it was agreed that I could have a month off, with the warning that this would not make me popular with the new editorial team.

Shrimsley asked me what I was going to do – and I told him I wanted to go to Normandy to brush up my French. He raised no objection; in fact I think he rather envied me.

My wonderful wife Robina, now the children were at school, had recently graduated in art from La Sainte Union des Sacrés Coeurs, the college being a short walk from our home in Southampton (her grandfather, W H Snape, had been a noted artist and a member of the Royal Academy, but had died tragically young) and she was now teaching at a school for special needs children.

So, come the Easter holidays, I was able to get away for a few weeks in a quiet seaside spot near Cherbourg.

The owner of the hotel in Barfleur took one look at the typewriter I was carrying and then showed me the small cottage across the square – far enough away not to disturb the hotel guests. I had the place to myself; coffee and croissants were brought across every morning, and I took my other meals in the hotel. I got through much of the first draft of the play – a farcical wedding with the comedy pointed at the impossibility of men and women living together in harmony.

A trio of Moroccan students came to energise my last week or so, insisting that I play football with them on the sandy beach. The artist among them produced a lightning portrait of me, which I still treasure.

Back home the warnings about the sabbatical annoying the new editorial team turned out to be spot on. I suddenly found that I was getting the cold shoulder on the subs' table. John Smythe (no doubt on instructions from above) stopped giving me work.

At lunch-time, everyone cleared off, none of them inviting me to join them in the pub. Was I supposed to break down in tears? Walk out, never to return?

What I did was to start making and receiving phone calls at my desk. There was plenty to do for the Regent Street Poly, or keeping in touch with my friends in showbiz, or following up stories for Southern Gas.

I could make all these calls legitimately: anything as long as I didn't talk to other newspapers, which could have got me sacked.

In fact I didn't do a hand's turn for the *NoW* for best part of a month and the only person on the subs' bench who spoke to me was the wonderful Monty Levy. Dear Mont, God bless him, insisted on keeping me company on the way to Waterloo every afternoon.

Towards the end of the month, I was chatting amiably on the phone to the editor of *Flame*, Frank Wiles, when Smythe's shadow loomed over me, in his hand a sturdy pair of scissors ...

Click. The phone went dead, the wire severed.

Smythe shoved a pile of copy in front of me. "Sort that story out for me, will you?" he said, and I was back on the job.

I stuck it out for a while, but by the summer of 1976 the only real contributions I was making was my copy-tasting stint on Saturdays, and the occasional story I picked up. I was moaning about this to Rosalie Shann over a drink one lunchtime.

She happened to be extolling the freedom and the virtues of being a freelance. Apart from the top-class stories she turned in for us, you were liable to find her by-line in popular magazines, especially those aimed at female readers.

"You ought to go freelance, John," she told me. "A good salary is all very well but have you considered this – when you are working for a single boss you are selling your time, which God knows is definitely a limited commodity. Whereas as a freelance you are selling talent: it's elastic and you can stretch it a lot wider. These days there's so many opportunities for decent writers. I mean look at the number of outlets you have already..."

I mentally ticked off all the work I was doing on the days when I was not at the *NoW*: Southern Gas, Delfont's sideshows, the occasional piece for *Hampshire* magazine, stints at the Poly and my newish connection with a magazine directed at independent decorators (many with surprisingly top-drawer clients, such as up-market hotels in London). They were running my column for this magazine under the banner:

JOHN BULL'S BRITAIN

You'd be surprised how many of the great and the good of British showbiz had worked as painters and decorators in earlier, hungry days, and were happy to tell me all about it: apparently it made fascinating reading to the other members of the trade.

I wasn't alone there, either. Another regular contributor to the magazine was *NoW* colleague David Roxan, our left-wing industrial correspondent. David was considered a mine of information in his field. Which reminds me, one time while I was chatting to his wife at a party, she entertained me – and soon a fascinated audience – about her life as a leading archaeologist.

"How does it work?" I asked.

"Oh it's like this – you spend all your working life getting to know more and more about less and less, until in the end you become the world's leading expert on one tiny field in Anatolia. Then you retire."

I followed up on Rosalie's advice over lunch with my tax advisors Kernon and Co. Pat Kernon – and later his son Barry – handled the tax affairs of just about everybody with a Fleet Street byline. In the foyer of their offices most of their clients' names were displayed in gold leaf, all followed by the magic word 'limited' – as in, for instance, *Michael Gabbert Ltd.* And so began a happy and often lucrative freelance life that lasted until I retired.

About this time Robina told me that her alma mater, La Sainte Union, had now qualified to award first degrees in the arts, under the aegis of the University of Southampton, and was advertising for suitable mature candidates. French Studies appealed to me, so I dropped a line to the principal, Sister Imelda Marie, who arranged for me to be interviewed by the head of department.

The interview was, of course, entirely in French and though my French was appalling, it was understandable – if you were a Paris guttersnipe. I usually tried to get round the problem by memorising a few unique and highly grammatical French phrases. This generally got a respectful response from the native .. and I'd take the sting out of the conversation with this little phrase entirely of my own creation:

"Merci, madame, vous êtes très gentile, j'aime beaucoup la langue française que je parle bien – jusqu'à l'ouverture de la bouche."

So the three-year BA course was there for the taking.

I had a long chat with Bernard Shrimsley and I got the impression he would have been happy to change places with me to spend his days in blissful, dreamy academe rather than in the nervous horror of pushing the *NoW* to the top of the sales figures. He promised to do what he could for me.

So it wasn't long before I resigned from full-time work at the paper – and the editorial department presented me with a set of French dictionaries at my farewell party. Some of them were rather surprised to see me return, a few weeks later, to my old seat on the back bench as copytaster – but as a Saturday freelance. They suggested I re-imburse them for their share of the leaving gift. Not likely.

14

A Heavy Blow

My course at La Sainte Union – LSU – began in October 1976. Along with about 20 fellow mature students, I was the guinea pig in an experiment: we were all studying European History and Literature, but half of us were combining this with French, and half with German. The total number of students at the college was nearly 700 – mostly young women.

I'd seen enough of the place through accompanying Robina to social events, so I knew some of the leading lights on the staff, especially Imelda Marie, possibly the most impressive women I've ever met. She had an easy manner with the students but she could be tough on the Roman Catholic hierarchy – not excluding on one occasion the Bishop himself. His sin was to criticise the Holy Mother for smoking in the assembly hall. Big mistake ... we had to pray for his soul afterwards.

Later that term, the French degree group all went over to Normandy to stay for a few weeks at a comfortable hostel, while we studied the French scholastic system – which meant dropping in on an infant school, then at a lycée, and finally on an older group studying hard to get to an Ecole Superieur – the crème de la crème of French education, the better ones easily the equivalent of Oxford or Cambridge.

Academic learning came fairly easily to me. As a young lad I had been fascinated by magic shows and conjurors – I had avidly read a monthly magazine called *Magic Monthly*, which often carried articles encouraging young lads to learn the tricks of the trade – and through shows at our local church hall, where I was the spotlight operator, I got to know a couple of magicians, who were kind enough to indulge me with some tips, the best of which was how to increase your memory skills. I picked up all kinds of gimmicks. For instance, at school, our Latin master used to set us 50 words to learn each week. This was easy-peasy for me and I came out top every time. When Mr Hunt investigated, I confessed that was learning memory tricks from a conjuror.

"Show me," he said. And I gave him a very easy example:

"On your list you have 'Ludo – I play' but I turn it round so it's 'I play – Ludo'. See, it's easier to remember. Then instead of 'Agricola – farmer', I turn that round too ..."

And I confess that Farmer Agricola is still one of my oldest acquaintances, whereas there are days when I have to think a bit what my own name is. Mr Hunt from then on called me Jimpy, after the boy magician in a *Daily Mirror* comic strip.

I used to follow lectures at LSU by making connecting sketches and shapes with relevant dates and names to link up the message to the brain, a sort of pathway to memory. At the age of 40 I needed all the memory help I could get. I shared the system with my contemporaries, Beth and Sue, but I don't think they needed it as much as I did. They left me standing in the finals.

One of the best things about LSU for me was the appointment of a new chaplain, Father Francis, a Benedictine monk from Downside Abbey, who became one of the most treasured of friends. I used to tell my pub pals that, being one of only a handful of male students in a college of several hundred young women, I was fed up with getting my bottom pinched black and blue – a complete fabrication of course, or it was until the day I was entertaining a visiting mate over coffee in the college hall, when out of the crowd a young nun sneaked up and actually did pinch my bum. Now I wonder what sort of bloke put her up to that? Couldn't have been a priest, could it? You're damn right it could. Thank you, Francis.

After Christmas Robina began to suffer from stabbing pains in her back, which – being a nurse – she put down to the undoubted stress of teaching the special needs children at Red Lodge School.

I finally persuaded her to see our GP who put her on a course of tablets, but sensibly laid down the law that if the pains persisted after some weeks, she should consult him, pronto.

That's how, on Easter Day 1977 (incidentally, her 41st birthday) she reported to the Royal South Hants Hospital for tests. Our daughter Yolanda with her boyfriend Paul Tollefson and I went along to keep her spirits up, leaving Bink to look after Michael, now aged 11. The hospital reported that they had found some internal problems and suggested Robina stay on a ward for further investigation.

This was a heavy blow to us all.

So my precious Robina moved into a women's ward at the South Hants – and I then embarked on a home regime of dealing with the many visitors, family and friends who wanted to see her, while trying to cope with two teenage daughters, who quite understandably didn't quite like the routine I instituted at home.

Then I had a brainwave. I hired a butler to help out.

Some years earlier, Robina had introduced me to an old school friend of hers, Stuart, a brilliant boy at school and as a technical student with the RAF. But recently he had a problem holding down a job; he'd started to drink seriously, suffered a difficult divorce, and generally gone to the dogs. Robina, his old pal, persuaded us and our friends to tolerate the guy because he was down on his luck. It was not easy.

But at least I figured in return for bed and board, running me around in his car and generally helping out, I would have more time to devote to Robina. Soon, Stuart was firmly embedded in the family.

He was famous for his nutty ideas. One day, our gang had gathered in the Bay Tree pub in the city centre, to discuss plans for a street party to celebrate the Queen's Silver Jubilee. Stuart started handing round dandelion stalks culled from the garden. He had already clipped holes in the stalks – more or less at

Imelda Marie meets the butler

random – and instructed some of us to put aside our beer mugs and try to get a note out of each stalk. When he was satisfied he'd got enough of a variety of notes going, he shuffled us all around according to pitch, and then lined six of us up ready to sound off. The idea was that he would point to us in turn and we would blow a note. Magically, after a few false starts, the unmistakable six-note rhythm of the National Anthem shrilled out. The rest of the customers cheered heartily.

The medics decided to operate on Robina for further investigation. I was at LSU a few days afterwards when I got the word to go to the South Hants Hospital. There – in a scene I shall never forget – the matron laid on me the heaviest word ever: there was absolutely no hope for Robina.

> *No hope for me, for her children, for the kids at the*
> *special school, and for her many supporters in the*
> *crusade for women's liberation ...*

They brought her home and I gave up all else but looking after her. We coped as best we could, trying to keep smiling, and carried on with our plans for the Queen's Jubilee street party. Since it was common knowledge that Robina would not be well enough to join the party, some of her pals suggested we might place her indoors at the big front window of our house – with a board across the sill to a table in the garden. A wonderful idea, which worked beautifully on Jubilee day.

Some of the gang knew the gravity of her situation, so there was some subdued conversation around the inevitable end to her illness. There were some solemn nods all around when our friend, eminent psychiatrist Albert Kushlick quietly observed: "Well, none of us know whether we'll still be around tomorrow or the next day."

Within a week we were to discover just how true those words were.

Albert's wife Jill and her friend Jan, wife of the playwright Trevor Griffiths – he wrote a very moving play for BBC TV, about his wife's ordeal with breast cancer – were invited to visit Cuba as part of their ongoing campaign for women's rights.

They were due to fly on Friday May 27, having joined an international Aeroflot flight from Frankfurt. The plane, in poor visibility, hit power lines at Havana airport and crashed, killing all but two of the 70 passengers.

The news broke on the Saturday while I was doing my copytasting shift at the *NoW* and handling bulletins about the crash. I remember the frustration of the long wait before the list of passenger names came up on the wire. Meanwhile I drafted quick notes about Jill and Jan, and alerted the news desk to the backgrounds of their famous husbands.

I've had some bad days in the news business, but that was one of the nastiest. Thank God for the help and support of Monty Levy and everyone in the Saturday crew.

Indeed, through all the long months of Robina's last illness my colleagues at the *News of* treated me with a kind of easy-going sympathy and some sad, stiff upperlip warmth and companionship. Something I'll never forget.

I tried to keep Robina at home with me despite the advice of the doctor and the understandable doubts of her mother and father. Robina's older sister Dee – herself a nurse – came up with the real answer. She negotiated a bed for Robina at the newly opened Countess Moutbatten Hospice on the outskirts of Southampton. The clincher was when the doctor in charge himself came to see me. A devout Roman Catholic, he gently persuaded me to let go – with the promise I could spend as much time as I wanted at her bedside.

And so it was. I was there every day; the children also were allowed to drop in for a brief stay. I recall that Robina and I watched a lot of TV together, something we'd rarely been able to do. Fittingly for a combative women's campaigner, the last event we shared was Virginia Wade's wonderful 1977 win at Wimbledon.

15

Dame Elisabeth is Waiting

Once the *Sun* had been launched successfully and was seen to be earning its bread, Rupert turned his attention to more lucrative aspects of the media. He was already doing well in the United States, having taken over the *New York Times* and a newsgroup in Texas – based on San Antonio.

So we didn't see or hear much of the guv'nor, apart from the occasional phone call from distant places. For me this usually happened on a Saturday night when I was doing the late shift on the back bench, often with the whole place in my hands.

I recall one sweltering midsummer night when the few duty reporters were sweating over their poker game and the print boys out in the composing room were stripped to the waist. I didn't go to look in the basement, but one or two of the circulation managers dropped by for a drink with me, having been down in the sweaty hell of the pressroom.

"They're in a mutinous mood down there," one confided, mopping his upper body with his shirt, "and I must say I don't blame them – it really is like something from hell."

So I wasn't surprised when a couple of heavies sent by the Imperial Father (the head of all the Fathers of the Chapel of the various unions) came up to my desk with their ultimatum. They began with the usual mode of address:

"What it is, John," ... and then into the crux: "The boys are threatening to walk out – it ain't right to ask blokes to sweat in this heat."

They didn't need to spell it out – I got the picture.

"Leave it with me," I told them. "There's only the late London run to do – I'll see what the big boss says."

And then I placed a few likely calls ... and got a pretty prompt response from Rupert.

"How's the printing going?" he asked and I told him there was only the late London to go, but that the lads were threatening to walk.

"What do you think?"

"It is a good paper this week," I told him. "Would be a pity to lose it. But it is pretty hot down there – basically they want me to fan them with fivers."

An amiable chuckle down the line ...

"Okay, give 'em the good news, then." So I did.

On another night turn I picked up a call from the switchboard:

"Some old lady on the line, mate, can you talk to her?"

"Hello, is that the News of the World?" Slight accent I couldn't quite place.

"Who's calling?"

"Mr Murdoch's mother, young man – can I speak to him?"

"Hello Dame Elisabeth, I'm sorry, he's not here just now. Where are you calling from?"

"I'm at Heathrow. I'm at the arrivals desk. I was expecting someone to collect me."

(Oh dear, oh dearie me ... this is the lady famous for her quotes, such as "I have never wasted a moment of my life.")

I asked her: "Would you be kind enough to hand the phone to the young woman on the desk, just for a moment please?"

"Heathrow arrivals. How can I help you? "

"Hello, this is John Bull on the News of the World night desk," I said. "The lady you have there is Dame Elisabeth Murdoch, our owner's mother. Could you please get someone in authority to take her to your very best VIP lounge and cosset her until I can get the office Rolls out to her?"

Panicky voice: "Certainly, sir. I'll take Dame Elisabeth to the royal suite and make sure she's well looked after."

Rupert's mother then came on the line and I carefully told her what was happening and that a car was on its way. I phoned down to the Rolls chauffeur and told him to stand by for a trip to Heathrow – and why.

Then I set about finding Rupert. I struck lucky and a few minutes later he was on the phone.

"Mr Murdoch, your mother has just phoned from Heathrow."

"Oh, Lord, I'm supposed to be there."

I told him what I'd done and he said he'd better phone the chauffeur to pick him up on the way.

There we go – my job safe. Until the next time anyway.

My Saturday shifts meant that now and again I had to stay on the desk until the last edition – the late London – was running on the machines. By tradition, the late night man was treated to a taxi home, no matter where he lived.

The *NoW* had a deal with a chauffeuring company. God knows what they charged because the round trip from Bouverie Street to Bull Hall (my house in Southampton) was at least 140 miles.

We used to leave at about 2am and depending on the traffic out of London, would arrive at my place sometime after 4.30am. I used to make some coffee and give the driver a tip before turning in.

One night was unforgettable.

It had been an exceptionally busy day; I was dead on my feet when I got into the cab and immediately dropped off on the rear seat. I awoke with a start to find myself staring at the glittering facade of a tall building – the Savoy Hotel, rear entrance. The driver muttered a number of excuses, which I ignored and I told him to get out of town on the road west.

I was deep down and snoring when the driver woke me up again: this time all I could see was trees all around – we were well out in the country.

"Where the hell are we, and why have you stopped?"

Sheepishly he confessed he'd run out of petrol. He fished a can out of the boot and said he'd thumb a ride to the nearest petrol station to fill up and then come back for me.

"Well you do what you like," I said, "but you won't find me here. I'm going to try to get a lift myself." With a mouthful of curses, I set off down the road.

I'd probably walked a mile when a car loomed up going my way. I raised a hopeful thumb in the headlights and to my amazement the car pulled up. I trotted happily up to the driver's window, and discovered the car held two women. Trip over, I thought – but no.

The older of the two spoke up: "Which paper are you from? And where are you going?"

Miraculously it turned out they were heading for Southampton Docks for a trip on the QE2. Also the younger lady was the fiancée of a bloke I knew on *The People.*

"How did you know I was a journalist?" I finally got around to asking. They both laughed. "Who else would be blundering about the A3 at 3am carrying a pile of Sunday papers?"

One Saturday, Bernard Shrimsley invited me to come into his office for a chat.

"I seem to have a problem," he said, handing over a copy of *Private Eye.*

Now I was fairly case-hardened to the *Eye.* I used to follow up some of the stories, in case John Field could comment on them. I soon gave up on that idea when I discovered how makee-uppee (a Fleet Street hacks' euphemism for invented scoops) their stories tended to be.

The piece Shrimsley showed me was written by that unhappy snob Auberon Waugh - a typical diatribe of insulting lies all aimed at Shrimsley.

"The thing is, should I sue him for slander?" he asked.

I pointed out that *Private Eye* and Waugh should be ignored by the *News of the World* as being beneath our contempt.

I also added that any damages from a court case might be dangerous: "If it were to be just a few hundred quid, it could look as if that's all you valued yourself at," I said. "By far better, Bernard, would be for you to pop over to the leather shop in

Fleet Street and borrow a horsewhip ... go round to the *Eye* and call the bugger out. Take a photographer with you. It works a treat, I promise you. A picture of him sneaking away will do the trick."

In his autobiography Waugh brags about his insults to Bernard Shrimsley and makes some grotesquely wrong remarks about the John Field column and the *News of the World.*

As a young cub reporter, it was dinned into me: "Remember, son, we never pitchfork the dead." The best I can say about the poor bugger was that he wrote one good novel – *Consider the Lilies.*

When Bernard left, he was followed by two editors, both of whom lasted less than a year. Then came a better bet in Derek Jameson, working-class, outspoken, and a good newspaper man.

Jameson and I got on very well, but never better than on a Saturday in April 1983.

I arrived at my usual place on the back bench to find the editor and several senior execs poring over several volumes of manuscript.

"Ah, just the man I need," Jameson told me. "Come and sit in on this."

'This' was copy from the feature about the Hitler Diaries, which the *Sunday Times* – then recently acquired by Rupert Murdoch – had started to run the previous week, convinced by a well-known academic that the documents were authentic. The idea was that the *News of the World* would carry parts of the diaries in its next edition.

Jameson was dubious about the authenticity of the stuff and he also knew that I had recently been brushing up on Hitler biographies for a play I was writing ('Ten Days That Shook The Kremlin') about Stalin and the German invasion of Russia in 1941.

"Take this lot upstairs to the library and give it a thorough once-over," he told me. "Take as long as you need, then let me know what you think."

I found a quiet corner of the library, and fortified by coffee from my friends up there, I started combing through the English translations. From the start, the so-called comments by the Fuhrer just didn't tally with the tone of the events of June 1941 that I had read in various accounts of the dialogue between Hitler and his staff – and the way Hitler tended to record his conversations.

At the end of the morning I went back down to the Big Room and handed the documents over to the editor.

"Very interesting," I said, "but I would not like my name attached to any attempt at authentication of this lot as being the work of Der Fuhrer."

"Good enough for me," said Derek. "Let's find a new front page lead."

And as it turned out, no-one else seemed to want to stick their neck out either and the *Sunday Times* ended up carrying an apology for being misled.

Derek Jameson later moved to radio, to host a popular show on Radio 2. It was like a speaking version of the *News of the World*.

My long association with the *News of the World* from paper boy (with handcart) to one of the last of what Derek Jameson called the 'hot metal men' came to a very fitting end with Murdoch's secretive shift of the editorial staff to the premises and plant he'd acquired at Wapping.

We hacks were not supposed to know this was a permanent shift to web offset printing, just that it was an 'experiment'. On that January Saturday we were ostensibly producing the paper as always in Bouverie Street – and not to know that an identical paper was printing at Wapping on new, computer-driven presses.

Some of the editorial staff had secretly shifted location, but we who were left at Bouverie Street were not supposed to notice. Some hope! We were journalists after all.

With the newly minted Wapping paper in our hands, layout designer Bric Wilkins and I repaired to the Peanut Parlour to conduct a wake for the old *NoW*. The paper looked cheap, shoddy, and like a poor imitation of the *Mirror*. We finished up sharing a cell at the Tower ... the Tower Hotel that is – though in my case it felt very like the other place.

I had no wish to go to work in Wapping, or work for this kind of paper, and so I was offered a pay-off – something like a month's pay for every year of service. That amounted to a year-and-a-half's pay at the current rate and I became a full-time freelance.

16

The Neat Apple

So there I was – a widower with two teenage girls and a 12-year-old boy. I had discovered that widowerhood, far from being lonely, tended to attract attention. Invitations to dinner came my way, but – slow on the uptake as I then was – it took me quite a while to notice that the invitations invariably included a 'spare' single lady, a friend of the hostess. And guess where I was always seated?

My bright daughters spotted the scam quicker than I did. They tried hard to keep a straight face when 'near' neighbours knocked on the door with a dish of 'a little something we thought we'd share with you.' Yolanda and Bink dubbed them The Apple Pie Ladies – and threatened to organise a whip-round among them – cash donations only!

The recreational side of my life narrowed down to a weekly drink with the boys, or dinner with Father Francis. On one occasion I invited him to join me at Ted's Taverna, and I called Ted Muscovia, the proprietor, to tell him I was bringing a guest and ask him to put three bottles of retsina on ice for us.

Unknown to me, Francis – not a man to leave anything to chance (he was a Benedictine, after all) also took it upon himself to instruct Ted to put three bottles of retsina on ice.

The only thing I remember about that hot summer evening is that we had to invite Ted to help us get through the wine. Strangely, and I don't know how it happened, I woke up with the dawn to find myself lying on the college lawn beneath the statue of Our Lady.

"I couldn't think what else to do with you," Francis told me later.

After a couple of false starts with totally unsuitable females, lovely though they were, I found myself paying more attention to Amanda, a redhead in her early twenties who I'd first met when she was in the public relations department of Southern Gas. By now she had been hired by one of the best PR men ever – Ken Bowden, who had a lively portfolio of clients including Cunard and Carrefour, the French giant bringing the concept of hypermarkets to the UK. Ken was always brimming with ideas: when asked to promote a Hungarian wine company, he sent out a Hungarian stamp to every wine journalist he could find, with a message saying 'write on the back of this stamp everything you know about Hungarian wine'.

One day, Amanda told me she was a Country and Western fan. She played rhythm guitar in her own country-rock band, a trio called Silvertown. Intrigued, I asked if I could pop in and catch the act, and so duly found myself early one evening heading for a somewhat rundown city centre pub, *The Lord Louis*, with one of my mates, the artist Larry Wakefield. Larry specialised in the female form – undressed, of course. In fact, I once got him on the front page of *The Guardian*, in a row where a fellow lecturer (female) objected to Larry's nudes that, until then, had taken pride of place in buildings throughout the campus of the University of Southampton.

As we ambled up to the bar and ordered a couple of pints, the band (all in cute Western gear) swung into a brisk rendition of *Johnny B Goode*.

Larry gave me a speculative look. "That for you, then?"

"Dunno," I said, "though it might be better to assume it was mere co-incidence."

Silvertown then changed the mood for a song called *Sunday Driver*, introduced by Amanda, written and sung by lead guitarist Diz Withers:

Mama hold on real tight now
Your boy is going on the run
With or without his right arm, honey
He's gonna have a lot of fun
You wrapped him up in something heavy
It could have been a ball and chain
He's doing his best to leave you
And you won't see him again.

His lyrics brought a nod of approval from Larry and a scattered round of applause from the half-dozen early-doors drinkers. Except for one guy, bearded and – though this was a warm evening – decked out in a scruffy duffel coat, an ancient scarf and a big pair of rubber boots. He started clapping in time to the beat, and interrupting now and again with 'Bring back the lassie ... bring her back ...'

Amanda and Diz took the hint and flowed into a quiet duet. The regulars settled down to enjoy it, but Old Father Time was still standing and waving his arms about. Then he knocked over a chair in the row in front of him, and tried to climb over the rest of the chairs to get to the stage.

The drummer upped the volume, people started stamping their feet and Larry shouted: "Where the hell is the bar staff?"

I started up the side of the room towards the stage and Larry, bless him, helped the old boy to his feet and handed him over to the barman, who dragged him to the nearest exit.

The band started packing up. The evening had run its course, but I did get the chanteuse to agree to come to dinner with me the following week.

I decided to make this date something special. Instead of phoning, I dropped in at a popular restaurant out in the sticks to make sure it would offer the right sort of atmosphere. The manager was impressed by the care I was taking, and the prelim was complete when I asked if he would place a gardenia at my guest's table place on the night.

It was a promising early autumn evening as I drove over to pick her up and then "Bong! Rattle, rattle ..." a front hubcap dropped off my Citroen Dyane. By the time I'd got the damn thing back on, my hands were black as the ace of spades. Great start.

Then I realised I was just a stone's throw from a pub. I parked, went in, said a cheery 'Evenin' all' and dived into the Gents to wash up. So I was more or less presentable at her door and almost on time. She was wearing a silky jade-coloured dress and a silver necklace. Later, when I introduced her to Stuart, my 'butler', he took to referring to her as the Neat Apple.

As we parked and entered the lounge bar of the restaurant, Marcel, the boss of the place, came hurrying over. Ignoring me, he grabbed hold of my date:

"Amanda – thank God you're here – I've been trying to phone you. The band for tonight have run their van into a ditch near Chichester. Have you got your guitar with you?"

Before I could open my mouth, Amanda had agreed to go home and get her guitar.

"By the way it's a double act," she said, "John here does the patter and introduces the numbers. We'll talk about the money when I get back." Then she took my car keys and hurried away.

Fleet Street prepares you for a lot of things, but to this day I do not want to recall the pain and torment of my 'performance'. We did get a very fine dinner though and finished the evening with a moonlight stroll along the seashore.

Apparently this was to be the start of a beautiful courtship. Months later, in a more intimate café, Amanda leant over the table and asked me to marry her.

I promptly answered 'YES', at the precise moment when she was attempting to spear her Chinese toffee banana dessert with her fork. A toffee banana went skidding across the room.

Later I went through the formal procedure of asking her father, Alan, for his daughter's hand. I subsequently learned that, after we went into another room for me to broach this serious business, leaving Amanda and her mother in the sitting room, Amanda had asked her mother if she could guess what I wanted to ask her father. 'Is he asking for a loan?' she said.

A family discussion concluded that we would be married in Gosport, where Amanda's parents lived, where I had grown up, and where we had both gone to school (give or take a 20-year age gap.)

Indeed, we were to be married at Holy Trinity Church, the most beautiful parish church in England (so everyone in Gosport says) and home to George Frederick Handel's organ, bought for him by the Duke of Chandos, and snapped up by the townsfolk of Gosport when the duke's estate was sold up. The Vicar of Holy Trinity, the long-serving John Capper, agreed to share the conducting of our marriage ceremony with Father Francis from La Sainte Union, thus neatly closing the gap between Anglo Catholicism and Roman Catholicism.

These two appeared on the day having vied with each other to deck themselves out in the most gorgeous robes they could get their hands on, in direct competition with my beautiful bride and my daughters, the glowing bridesmaids. My son, the best man, and I ... well, we did our best in stiff hired suits.

The bride was delighted to find that instead of flying to the US on honeymoon, as she had thought we were going to do, we were booked to sail to New York in the QE2. And we were to be guests at the Captain's Table.

It turned out that the ship's master for that crossing was Capt Bob Arnott, who was as amazed to see her as she was to see him. In her PR role for Cunard she had played a major behind-the-scenes part in an episode of the popular Thames Television show *This is Your Life*, presented by Eamonn Andrews, in which it was Bob Arnott who would be surprised by the 'Big Red Book'. It had meant hiding away the TV celebrity on board before the show. She had had the bright idea of tucking him away in the ladies toilets, where she regaled him with stories about how, as a small girl, she had loved *Crackerjack* and had written a fan letter to him when she was five years old. Perhaps not the best chat-up line in the world.

17

A Burst of Colour

I t wasn't quite the end of Fleet Street for me.
Out of the blue, in 1986, Michael Gabbert dropped in on me
at Bull Hall. He lit up a cigar that put me in mind of the thick
end of a billiard cue and announced:

"We've pulled a few strokes in our time, you and me. How
about one last big one before we roll over? Be nice to go out
with a bang."

And that was how we came to liven up a dying Fleet Street
with the lightning success of *Sunday Sport.*

The adult mag publisher David Sullivan had commissioned
a survey of newspaper readership – and discovered there
were some nine million people out there who never bought
a newspaper at all. So in partnership with the Gold brothers,
publishers and owners of the Ann Summers sex toys empire,
he set about launching the *Sport* to scoop up these punters.
Sullivan had started his entrepreneurial career early: buying
bundles of stamps and selling them to his schoolmates. Before
long, he was selling soft porn photos, adult magazines and blue
movies: he was a millionaire before he was 25.

The *Sport* was a good idea, but the TV companies refused to
run his sexy ads, and some newsagents – W H Smith for instance
– said they wouldn't stock it (though they caved in when it was
so successful) and Sullivan soon found his first choice of editor
was rather off the mark.

Which is where Mr Gabbert came in. By this time he had
a Saturday night radio show on a regional BBC station (four
hours of him talking – not a difficult task for him), so had only

Sports editor Tony Flood (right)
seeing off the pages on a Saturday

Me, listening to Tony in full flood

limited time to head up the *Sport* for David Sullivan. What he was able to do, however, was to blag his way into the studios of radio stations up and down the country, with the great message of a *'coming shortly'* newspaper dedicated to the neglected non-reader in the pub.

One of Gabbert's first coups was the recruiting of Bobby Moore as sports editor. Bobby, hailed as England's greatest footballer, had been the captain of the 1966 England team that won the Holy Grail of every supporter's dream. Bobby was Mr Nice Guy writ large and his weekly column for the paper won over England's army of football worshippers. The new paper devoted more than half its 40-plus pages to sport – football, American football, and horse racing – and ran a successful campaign to change the rules to allow racing on Sundays in the UK, a long-cherished crusade by David Sullivan.

After I spent a few months as a casual sub-editor at the leaky old building by the canal at Islington, getting the feel of the show, I was appointed editor.

The casual shifts had given me the chance to work out the pros and cons of the *Sport* – and in my first week in the editor's chair, I managed to cut our outgoings by some £70,000 a year. For instance, American football was then vastly popular on TV in the UK, but our sports team were paying far too much for pictures of the stars like The Fridge and Good Time Tommy Landry. I talked to Channel 4, who had exclusive UK rights to the games and – in return for the promise of a full double-page spread every week – they were only too happy to send us pictures for free.

One of *Sunday Sport's* best assets was our baby-faced newspaper designer Drew Robertson, youngest of a solid newspaper family. With the new technology, newspapers were able to print colour pictures (hallelujah!) but these had not got beyond the rectangular boxes of the early computer layouts. Drew was quick to follow a popular Irish Sunday paper, which had the nerve to use pictures that 'broke the frame', a shock-and-awe technique that the public had never seen before except in American comic strips – and a revolution in full colour was underway.

Michael Gabbert - in control

We were getting a lot of flak from women's groups for our saucy bums-and-boobs pix, and our reporters investigated some of the protesters, who were no better than they should be. One group announced they were going to kidnap the editor, so we ran a story about my bodyguard (actually my secretary's boyfriend Bob, a really peace-loving guy.) Gabbert and I ordered that they all be left alone: as things stood they were giving us some very necessary publicity.

I appointed Rab Anderson, a canny Scot who revelled in every trick in the book, as news editor – and the kind of stories we wanted really started to flow in. One of his specialities was using stories from our freelance stringers and then selling them on to foreign papers for a nice profit.

Rab opened a separate bank account with the aid of Mr Sullivan's moneywise assistant who had a desk in our office. When Sullivan queried this 'rogue' account, Rab assured him that this was general practice in Fleet Street. It provided a source of ready money in case we needed to grab an offer of a must-have story without possible crucial delay waiting for cash.

"It's still your money," Rab told him. "And actually there's quite a lot there."

It's hard to think of a stunt we didn't pull in those early days. For instance we had horse-racing 'Tips from Beyond the Grave', the back-story being that we'd hired a spirit medium to get in touch with one of the greatest jockeys of all time, Fred Archer – well if he couldn't pick 'em, who could?

Later we had my mother on the payroll with 'MUM'S TIPS'. I used to phone her on Saturday morning for her selection. She was never a threat to our Fleet Street tipsters, but over time she did come up with some useful combination bets.

My son Michael was editing a weekly paper in Portsmouth, but he used to join us to lend a hand when he could and he blagged his sisters into contributing an agony aunt column, 'Dear Nikki', that quickly picked up a big postbag.

We had two young girl reporters who covered the celebrity circuit with flair and a nose for news (both later found top jobs in the media) but my one disappointment was a young lad with a gift for the off-beat 'scoop.' He used to amuse us by commuting to work on a unicycle. Imagine my disappointment when he failed to show up one day, leaving a telephone message to say he'd quit newspapers for higher education – to be exact, a job with a circus.

Then, true to form, Rab came up with a real circulation builder. He ran a promotion for pubs to join in a Sunday lunchtime offer – "Buy a copy of *Sunday Sport* and get a free pint from the landlord."

We carried the offer on the front page and listed the signed-up pubs in a small panel inside. In no time we were running a full column of pubs in London, with other pubs over the country clamouring to join in.

Sunday Sport had started out being banned from TV advertising altogether, but the smash-hit satirical programme on ITV, the totally irreverent *Spitting Image*, did us the favour of a lifetime.

I tuned in one Sunday and there we were – Rab and me, two glorious pigs in dirty macs, discussing ideas for the *Sport*. Their chat was mysteriously accurate, we thought. And later, when the credits rolled, we realised that at least one of the listed scriptwriters was on our payroll.

We had started out with the paper being printed by the provincial evening papers in Northampton (serving the midlands) and Portsmouth (serving the south) – and later we virtually doubled the circulation by adding another printing press, belonging to the local evening paper in Blackburn, to serve the north of the country and – importantly – thousands of Scottish readers.

The *Sport* editorial team moved from London to Northampton on Saturdays, where the sports pages and any late stories were compiled. My predecessor had organised a helicopter company to fly the printing 'plates' – once they'd been used on the Northampton presses – down to Portsmouth for the second printing. The trouble was that the whirlybirds could not fly in even slightly bad weather, so I hired a flying club at Northampton to do the job with a light aircraft.

I volunteered to do the first run to Southampton airport, where my wife would be waiting on the runway to drive me and the plates down to Portsmouth. I joined the pilot in the two-seater plane and we took off in the late afternoon sunshine. After I got bored with the views, I said to the pilot: "What happens if you suddenly have a heart attack, Mike?"

He squinted across at me to see if I was serious.

"Well if you are into survival I can give you a few tips. Get a grip on that wheel ..."

A typical Sunday Sport front page

The world outside rolled through 90 degrees and the land moved up outside my window.

Mike told me that this was because I was now flying the plane. And he explained what I had to do.

The lights of evening were just coming on below.

"Turn left and follow the motorway," he said.

And that's how I cruised the Cessna down over the M27 to Eastleigh. In the glow of dusk, Southampton airport rose slowly up to meet us.

Mike said: "You'd better let me take over – this is a wonderful aircraft, but your chances of landing in the dusk are rather less than nil."

He was obviously not a risk-taker. I remember thinking he'd never make the grade on *Sunday Sport.*

In seven months we had increased the sales from next-to-nothing to half a million, on a 30p per copy sale.

The Observer was first to notice that *Sunday Sport* had turned into something rather more than just a joke and ran a full-page feature on me and my crew. And Mr Murdoch was not best pleased to find his ex-figleaf was grabbing something like 300,000 copies off the *News of the World* every Sunday.

Ten years later *The Observer* carried my happy recollections of the *Sport* phenomenon and its influence, good or bad, on the tabloid world. What it adds up to is this: if the Sunday newsstands smack you in the eye with a blaze of colour, s'all my fault. I finally dropped the figleaf.

Late Final

I set out to write my memories of the wonderful, scurrilous, exciting, laughable, hilarious years I spent in Fleet Street, dipped deep in ink and sheer excitement.

On reading it all through again, it hit me – what I had written was simply an epitaph to Fleet Street. So be it ... God bless 'em all.